Sociolinguistics:
An Introduction

Peter Trudgill

Penguin Books

Penguin Books Ltd, Harmondsworth,
Middlesex, England
Penguin Books Inc., 7110 Ambassador Road,
Baltimore, Maryland 21207, U.S.A.
Penguin Books Australia Ltd, Ringwood,
Victoria, Australia
Penguin Books Canada Ltd,
41 Steelcase Road West, Markham, Ontario, Canada
Penguin Books (N.Z.) Ltd,
182–190 Wairau Road, Auckland 10, New Zealand

First published 1974
Copyright © Peter Trudgill, 1974

Made and printed in Great Britain by
Hazell Watson & Viney Ltd,
Aylesbury, Bucks.
Set in Monotype Times

Contents

Figures, Maps and Tables

Acknowledgements

A book of this type necessarily draws rather heavily on the work of others. I have made use of the publications of the following scholars without acknowledgement in the text: P. van den Berghe, C. Geertz, T. Hill, K. Kazazis, R. Keller, L. Lanham, W. Lockwood, S. Martin, W. McCormack, J. Ornstein, E. Polomé, J. Rubin and W. Stewart. I would like also to acknowledge the help I have had with translations from Ron Brasington, Arne Kjell Foldvik, Viviane Schumacher, and Spanish students at the University of Reading, as well as the invaluable information I have received from Malcolm Petyt, Dubravka Lazić Yarwood, Greek friends, and many other colleagues, students and friends in Reading and elsewhere. I am especially grateful to David Crystal for his help and advice with the book as a whole, and to Jill Tozer for typing it. Thanks are also due to Viv Edwards, Paul Fletcher and Mike Garman for help with the proofs.

Phonetic Symbols

č	*ch*ew
ç	German i*ch*, Scots ni*cht*, RP* *hu*ge
ḍ	retroflex† d
ð	*th*is
g	*g*uy
j	*y*ou
ǰ	*j*ust
ḷ	retroflex l
ʈ	retroflex flap, as in some Indian languages and some types of Swedish and Norwegian
ṇ	retroflex n
ṇ̩	syllabic nasal
ŋ	si*ng*
ɹ	RP *r*ow
R	French *r*ose
š	*sh*e
θ	*th*ing
x	German na*ch*, Scots lo*ch*, Spanish ba*j*o
ž	vi*si*on
ʔ	a glottal stop, e.g. 'cockney' *better* 'be'er'
ʕ	pharyngeal fricative, as in Arabic
a	French p*a*tte, North of England p*a*t, Australian p*a*rt
ɑ	RP p*a*th, p*a*rt

---

* For the term *RP*, see p. 19.
† For the term *retroflex,* see p. 164.

12 Phonetic Symbols

æ	RP p*at*
e	Scots *a*te, French *et*
ɛ	RP b*e*d
ə	*a*bout
ɜ	RP b*ir*d (Note: no [r])
i	RP *ea*t, French *i*l
ɪ	RP *i*t
o	French *eau*, Scots n*o*
ɔ	RP l*aw*
ɵ	a central vowel between ø and o
ɒ	RP *o*n
ø	French *eux*, German b*ö*se
u	RP f*oo*l, French *ou*
ʊ	RP p*u*ll
ʉ	a central vowel between [y] and [u], cf. Scots 'h*oo*se'
ʌ	RP *u*p
y	French t*u*, German *ü*ber
~	vowel nasalized, e.g. õ
₊	vowel fronted, e.g. o̟
·	vowel raised, e.g. o̩
ꞏ	long vowel, e.g. oꞏ

Brackets [ ] indicate phonetic transcription;
oblique dashes / /, phonemic transcription.

1. Sociolinguistics – Language and Society

Everyone knows what is supposed to happen when two Englishmen who have never met before come face to face in a railway compartment – they start talking about the weather. In some cases this may simply be because they happen to find the subject interesting. Most people, though, are not particularly interested in analyses of climatic conditions, so there must be other reasons for conversations of this kind. One explanation is that it can often be quite embarrassing to be alone in the company of someone you are not acquainted with and *not* speak to them. If no conversation takes place the atmosphere can become rather strained. However, by talking to the other person about some neutral topic like the weather, it is possible to strike up a relationship with him without actually having to say very much. Railway-compartment conversations of this kind – and they do happen, although not of course as often as the popular myth supposes – are a good example of the sort of important social function that is often fulfilled by language. Language is not simply a means of communicating information – about the weather or any other subject. It is also a very important means of establishing and maintaining relationships with other people. Probably the most important thing about the conversation between our two Englishmen is not the words they are using, but the fact that they are talking at all.

There is also a second explanation. It is quite possible that the first Englishman, probably subconsciously, would like to get to know certain things about the second – for instance what sort of job he does and what social status he has. Without this kind of information he will not be sure exactly how he should behave towards him. He can, of course, make intelligent guesses about his companion from the sort of clothes he is wearing, and other visual clues, but he can hardly ask him direct questions about his social background, at least not at this stage of the relationship. What he *can* do – and any reasoning along these lines on his part is again usually subconscious – is to engage him in conversation. He is then likely to find out certain things about the other person quite easily. He will learn these things not so much from what the other man says as from *how he says it*, for whenever we speak we cannot avoid giving our listeners clues about our origins and the sort of person we are. Our accent and our speech generally show what part of the country we come from, and what sort of background we have. We may even give some indication of certain of our ideas and attitudes, and all of this information can be used by the people we are speaking with to help them formulate an opinion about us.

These two aspects of language behaviour are very important from a social point of view: first, the function of language in establishing social relationships; and, second, the role played by language in conveying information about the speaker. We shall concentrate for the moment on the second 'clue-bearing' role, but it is clear that both these aspects of linguistic behaviour are reflections of the fact that there is a close inter-relationship between language and society.

In seeking clues about his companion the Englishman is making use of the way in which people from different social and geographical backgrounds use different kinds of language. If the second Englishman comes from Norfolk, for example, he will probably use the kind of language spoken by people from that part of the country. If he is also a middle-class businessman, he will use the kind of language associated with men of this type. 'Kinds of language' of this sort are often referred to as *dialects*, the first type in this case being a regional dialect and the second a social dialect. The term *dialect* is a familiar one and most people will think that they have a good idea of what it means. In fact, though, it is not a particularly easy term to define – and this also goes for the two other commonly used terms which we have already mentioned, *language* and *accent*.

Let us confine our attention for the moment to the terms *dialect* and *language*. Neither represents a particularly clear-cut or watertight concept. As far as *dialect* is concerned, for example, it is possible to speak of 'the Norfolk dialect' or 'the Suffolk dialect'. On the other hand, one can also talk of more than one 'Norfolk dialect' – 'East Norfolk' or 'South Norfolk', for instance. Nor is the distinction between 'Norfolk dialect' and 'Suffolk dialect' so straightforward as one might think. If you travel from Norfolk into Suffolk, investigating conservative rural dialects as you go, you will find, at least at some points, that the linguistic characteristics of these dialects change *gradually* from place to place. There is no clear *linguistic* break between Norfolk and Suffolk dialects. It is not possible to state in linguistic terms where people stop speaking Norfolk dialect and start speaking Suffolk dialect. If we choose to place the dividing line between the two at the county boundary, then we are basing our decision on *social* (in this case local-government–political) rather than on linguistic facts.

The same sort of problem arises with the term *language*. For example, Dutch and German are known to be two distinct languages. However, at some places along the Dutch–German frontier the dialects spoken on either side of the border are extremely similar. If we choose to say that people on one side of the border speak German and those on the other Dutch, our choice is again based on social and political rather than linguistic factors. This point is further emphasized by the fact that the ability of speakers from either side of the border to understand each other will often be considerably greater than that of German speakers from this area to understand speakers of other German dialects from distant parts of Austria or Switzerland. Now, in attempting to decide which language someone is speaking, we *could* say that if two speakers cannot understand one another, then they are speaking different languages. Similarly, if they *can* understand each other, we could say that they are speaking dialects of the *same* language. Clearly, however, this would lead to some rather strange results in the case of Dutch and German, and indeed in many other cases.

The criterion of 'mutual intelligibility', and other purely

linguistic criteria, are, therefore, of less importance in the use of the terms *language* and *dialect* than are political and cultural factors of which the two most important are *autonomy* and *heteronomy*. We can say that Dutch and German are *autonomous*, since both are independent, standardized varieties of language with, as it were, a life of their own. On the other hand, the non-standard dialects of Germany, Austria and German-speaking Switzerland are all *heteronomous* with respect to standard German, in spite of the fact that they may be very unlike each other and that some of them may be very like Dutch dialects. This is because speakers of these German dialects look to German as their standard language, read and write in German, and listen to German on radio and television. Speakers of dialects on the Dutch side of the border, in the same way, will read newspapers and write letters in Dutch, and any standardizing changes that occur in their dialects will take place in the direction of standard Dutch, not standard German.

A more extreme case which illustrates the sociopolitical nature of these two terms can be taken from Scandinavia. Norwegian, Swedish and Danish are all autonomous, standard languages, corresponding to three distinct nation states. Educated speakers of all three, however, can communicate freely with each other. But in spite of this mutual intelligibility, it would not make sense to say that Norwegian, Swedish and Danish are really the same language. This would constitute a direct contradiction of the political and cultural facts.

This discussion of the difficulty of using purely linguistic criteria to divide up varieties of language into distinct languages or dialects is our first encounter with a problem very common in the study of language and society – the problem of *discreteness* and *continuity*, of whether the division of linguistic and social phenomena into separate entities has any basis in reality, or is merely a convenient fiction. It is as well to point out that this *is* a problem since terms like 'cockney', 'Brooklynese', 'Yorkshire accent', 'Negro dialect' are frequently used as if they were self-evident, self-contained discrete varieties with well-defined, obvious characteristics. It is often convenient to talk as if this were the case, but it should always be borne in mind that the true picture may very well be considerably more complex than this. We can talk, for example, about 'Canadian English' and 'American English' as if they were two clearly distinct entities, but it is in fact very difficult to find any single linguistic feature which is common to all varieties of Canadian English and not present in any variety of American English.

If we at this point return to purely linguistic facts, a further distinction now needs to be made. The term *dialect* refers, strictly speaking, to differences between kinds of language which are differences of vocabulary and grammar as well as pronunciation. The term *accent*, on the other hand, refers solely to differences of pronunciation, and it is often important to distinguish clearly between the two. This is particularly true, in the context of English, in the case of the dialect known as *standard English*. In many important respects this dialect is different from other English dialects, and some people may find it surprising to see it referred to as a dialect at all. However, in so far as it differs grammatically and lexically from other varieties of English, it *is* legitimate to consider it a dialect: the term *dialect* can be used to apply to all varieties, not just to non-standard varieties. (Note that we shall be employing *variety* as a neutral term to apply to any 'kind of language' we wish to talk about without being specific.)

Standard English is that variety of English which is usually used in print, and which is normally taught in schools and to non-native speakers learning the language. It is also the variety which is normally spoken by educated people and used in news broadcasts and other similar situations. The difference between standard and non-standard, it should be noted, has nothing in principle to do with differences between formal and colloquial language, or with concepts such as 'bad language'. Standard English has colloquial as well as formal variants, and standard English speakers swear as much as others. (It is worth pointing this out because many people appear to believe that if someone uses slang expressions or informal turns of phrase this means that he is not speaking standard English.) Historically speaking, the standard language developed out of the English dialects used in and around London as these were modified through the centuries by speakers at the court, by scholars from the universities and other writers, and, later on, by the public schools. As time passed, the English used in the upper classes of society in the capital city came to diverge quite markedly from that used by other social groups and came to be regarded as the model for all those who wished to speak and write well. When printing became widespread, it was inevitably the form of English most widely used in books, and, although it has undergone many changes, it has always retained its character as the most widely accepted form of the English language.

Within standard English there are a small number of regional differences which tend to attract attention. Standard Scottish English is not exactly the same as standard English English, for example, and standard American English is somewhat different again. The differences include some well-known vocabulary items, such as British *lift*, American *elevator*, and some grammatical details:

> British: *I have got*
> American: *I have gotten*
> English: *It needs washing*.
> Scottish: *It needs washed*.

There are also a number of other variations associated with smaller regions such as, say, parts of the North and Midlands of England as opposed to the South:

> North: *You need your hair cutting*.
> South: *You need your hair cut*.

Generally speaking, however, standard English has a widely accepted, codified grammar and vocabulary. There is a general consensus among educated people, and in particular amongst those who hold powerful and influential positions, as to what is standard English and what is not – standard English is, as it were, imposed from above over the range of regional dialects, and for this reason can be called a *superposed variety* of language.

This general consensus, however, does not apply to pronunciation. There is no universally acknowledged standard accent for English, and it is, at least in theory, possible to speak standard English with any regional or social accent. (In practice there are some accents, generally very localized accents associated with groups who have had relatively little education, which do not frequently occur together with standard English, but there is no necessary connection between standard English and any particular accent or accents.) There is also one accent which *only* occurs together with standard English. This is the British English accent, or more properly the English English accent, which is known to linguists as R P ('received pronunciation'). This is the accent which developed largely in the English public schools, and which was until recently required of all BBC announcers. It is known colloquially under various names such as 'Oxford English' and 'BBC English', and is still the accent taught to non-native speakers learning British pronunciation.

R P is unusual in that the relatively very small numbers of speakers who use it do not identify themselves as coming from any particular geographical region. R P is largely confined to England, although it also has prestige in the rest of the British Isles (as well as in Australia, New Zealand, South Africa, and parts of Canada), but this is the only extent to which it is localized. As far as England is concerned, R P is a *non-localized* accent. It is, however, not necessary to speak R P to speak standard English. Standard English can be spoken with any regional accent, and in the vast majority of cases normally is.

Because language as a social phenomenon is closely tied up with the social structure and value systems of society, different dialects and accents are evaluated in different ways. Standard English, for example, has much more status and prestige than any other English dialect. It is a dialect that is highly valued by many people, and certain economic, social and political benefits tend to accrue to those who speak and write it. The R P accent also has very high prestige, as do certain American accents. In fact the 'conventional wisdom' of most English-speaking communities goes further than this. So statusful are standard English and the prestige accents that they are widely considered to be 'correct', 'beautiful', 'nice', 'pure' and so on. Other non-standard, non-prestige varieties are often held to be 'wrong', 'ugly', 'corrupt' or 'lazy'. Standard English, moreover, is frequently considered to be *the* English language, which inevitably leads to the view that other varieties of English are some kind of deviation from a norm, the deviation being due to laziness, ignorance or lack of intelligence. In this way millions of people who have English as their mother-tongue are persuaded that they 'can't speak English'.

The fact is, however, that standard English is only one variety among many, although a peculiarly important one. Linguistically speaking, it cannot even legitimately be considered *better* than other varieties. The scientific study of language has convinced most scholars that *all* languages, and correspondingly *all* dialects, are equally 'good' as linguistic systems. All varieties of a language are structured, complex, rule-governed systems which are wholly adequate for the needs of their speakers. It follows that value judgements concerning the correctness and purity of linguistic varieties are *social* rather than linguistic. There is nothing at all inherent in non-standard varieties which makes them inferior. Any apparent inferiority is due only to their association with speakers from under-privileged, low-status groups. In other words, attitudes towards non-standard dialects are attitudes which reflect the social structure of society. In the same way, societal *values* may also be reflected in judgements concerning linguistic varieties. For example, it is quite common in heavily urbanized Britain for rural accents, such as those of Devonshire, Northumberland or the Scottish Highlands, to be considered pleasant, charming, quaint or amusing. Urban accents, on the other hand, such as those of Birmingham, Newcastle or London, are often thought to be ugly, careless or unpleasant. This type of attitude towards rural speech is not so widespread in the United States, and this difference may well reflect the different way in which rural life is evaluated in the two countries.

The following example illustrates the extent to which judgements concerning the correctness and purity of linguistic varieties and features are social rather than linguistic. All accents of English have an /r/ sound in words such as *rat* and *rich* and most have an /r/ in *carry*, *sorry*. On the other hand there are a number of accents which have no /r/ in words like *cart* and *car*. These words formerly had an /r/ sound, as the spelling shows, but in these accents /r/ has been lost except where it occurs before a vowel. The /r/ in other contexts – at the end of a word (*car*) or before a consonant (*cart*) – can be referred to as 'postvocalic /r/'. (This term is not strictly accurate since it really means 'r after a vowel', which also applies to *carry*, but its use is widespread, and we shall continue to use it here.) Accents which lack postvocalic /r/ include a number in the United States and West Indies, many in England, Wales and New Zealand, and all in Australia and South Africa. In these accents pairs of words like *ma* and *mar* are pronounced in exactly the same way. Now, if we compare the accents of England and America with respect to this feature, one striking fact emerges. In England, other things being equal, accents *without* postvocalic /r/ have more status and are considered more 'correct' than accents *with*. RP, the prestige accent, does not have this /r/, and postvocalic /r/ is often used on radio, television and in the theatre to indicate that a character is rural, uneducated or both – one frequently hears it employed for comic effect in radio comedy series. On the other hand, although the situation in the United States is more complex, there are parts of the country where the exact reverse is true. In New York City, other things being equal, accents *with* postvocalic /r/ have more prestige and are considered more 'correct' than those without. The pronunciation of words like *car* and *cart* without an /r/ is socially stigmatized, and generally speaking, the higher up the social scale a speaker is, the more postvocalic /r/s he is likely to use. In English towns where both types of pronunciation can be heard, such as Bristol and Reading, this pattern is completely reversed. In other words, value judgements about language are, from a linguistic point of view, completely arbitrary. There is nothing inherent in postvocalic /r/ that is good or bad, right or wrong, sophisticated or uncultured. Judgements of this kind are social judgements based on the social connotations that a particular feature has in the area in question.

The fact that this is so, however, does not mean that linguists do not acknowledge that society evaluates different linguistic varieties in different ways. Linguistic descriptions note the appropriateness (rather than the 'correctness') of varieties for different contexts, and foreign-language teaching programmes are usually developed to teach the learner the standard variety of a language. At the same time, an increasing number of linguists are suggesting that the kind of attitude discussed above can in some cases be harmful. For example, it might have undesirable socio-psychological and pedagogical consequences if teachers involved in teaching standard English to speakers of non-standard varieties appear hostile towards their pupil's speech (see pp. 55 and 80).

Linguists also pay attention to subjective attitudes towards language for other reasons. They are important, for example, in the study of linguistic change, and can often help to explain why a dialect changes when and how it does. A recent investigation into the speech of New York City has shown that since the Second World War postvocalic /r/ has been very much on the increase in the city in the speech of the upper middle class. The impetus for this change may have come from the influx into the city during the war of many speakers from areas where postvocalic /r/ was a standard or prestige feature, but the change is more clearly due to a related shift in subjective attitudes towards pronunciations of this type on the part of all New York City speakers. During the course of the investigation tests were carried out on the informants' subjective attitudes in order to see if they reacted to postvocalic /r/ as a prestige feature. Those whose response indicated that for them /r/ was a prestige marker were labelled 'r-positive'. Table 1 shows the percentage of upper middle-class

Table 1. Attitudes towards and use of postvocalic /r/: upper middle class in New York City

age	% r-positive informants	% /r/ used
8–19	100	48
20–39	100	34
40+	62	9

speakers in three age-groups who were 'r-positive' together with the average percentage of postvocalic /r/s used in normal speech by the same three groups. It can be seen that for speakers aged under forty there has been a sharp increase in the favourable evaluation of postvocalic /r/. There has, correspondingly, been an even sharper increase in the use of this /r/ amongst younger speakers. Other evidence suggests that the change in subjective attitudes has been the cause rather than the effect of the change. The change in subjective attitudes, that is, has led to a change in speech patterns, although it is in fact only the upper middle class which has made a significant change in its speech.

Subjective attitudes towards linguistic forms do not always have this kind of effect. The above example illustrates that if a certain pronunciation comes to be regarded as a prestige feature in a particular community, then it will tend to be exaggerated. This kind of process can also take place in the opposite direction. On Martha's Vineyard, formerly a relatively isolated island off the coast of New England, fairly dramatic social changes have been taking place as a result of the increasing number of holiday-makers who come to the island in the summer months. These social changes have had linguistic consequences. Investigations have shown that the vowel sound of words such as *house*, *mouth*, *loud* has two different types of pronunciation on the island. (This also applies to the pronunciation of words like *ride* and *right*.) One is a low-prestige, old-fashioned pronunciation typical of the island, approximately [həus], with the first element of the diphthong resembling the vowel in *shirt* or the first vowel in *about*, [əbaut]. The second pronunciation is more recent on the island, and resembles more closely the vowel found in RP and some mainland American prestige accents: [haus], [əbaut]. Strangely enough, work carried out during the past decade or so has shown that the 'old-fashioned' form appears to be on the increase. The [əu] pronunciation is becoming exaggerated, and is occurring more frequently in the speech of more people. It has emerged that this linguistic change is due to the subjective attitudes speakers on the island have towards this linguistic form. Natives of the island have come to resent the mass invasion of outsiders and the change and economic exploitation that go with it. So those people who most closely identify with the island way of life have begun to exaggerate the typical island pronunciation, in order to signal their separate social and cultural identity, and to underline their belief in the old values. This means that the 'old-fashioned' pronunciation is in fact most prevalent amongst certain sections of the younger community. The tendency is most marked amongst young people who have left to work on the mainland *and have come back* – having rejected the mainland way of life. It is least marked amongst those who have ambitions to settle on the mainland. This process is to a certain extent a conscious one in that speakers are aware of the fact that the island accent is different, but the awareness does not extend to recognition of the significance of the diphthong itself. Unconsciously, however, speakers are aware of the social significance of this pronunciation, and their attitudes towards it are favourable because of their social attitudes. In other words, linguistic change does not always take place in the direction of the prestige norm. On the contrary, all sorts of other attitudes towards language have to be taken into consideration. Language can be a very important factor in group identification, group solidarity and the signalling of difference, and when a group is under attack from outside, signals of difference may become more important and are therefore exaggerated.

In the following chapters we shall examine some of the complex inter-relationships between language and society, of which subjective attitudes are just one facet. These inter-relationships take many forms. In most cases we shall be dealing with the *co-variation* of linguistic and social phenomena. In some cases, however, it makes more sense to consider that the relationship is in one direction only – the influence of society on language, or vice versa. We can begin with an example of this one-way relationship which supposedly involves the effect of language on society. There is a view, developed in various forms by different linguists, which is most frequently referred to as the 'Sapir–Whorf hypothesis', after the two linguists, Edward Sapir and Benjamin Lee Whorf, with whose names it is most often associated. The hypothesis is approximately that a speaker's native language sets up a series of categories which act as a kind of grid through which he perceives the world, and which constrain the way in which he categorizes and conceptualizes different phenomena. A language can affect a society by influencing or even controlling the world-view of its speakers. Most languages of European origin are very similar in this respect, presumably because of their common genetic relationship and the long cultural contact between them; the world-views of their speakers and their societies are perhaps for that reason not at all dissimilar. If, therefore, linguistic differences *can* produce cognitive differences, we shall have to demonstrate this by a comparison of sets of very different culturally separated languages.

European languages, for example, make use of tenses. Their usage is by no means identical, but it is usually not too difficult to translate, say, an English form into its equivalent in French or German. Some American Indian languages, on the other hand, do not have tenses, at least not as we know them. They may, however, distinguish in their verb forms between different kinds of activity which European speakers would have to indicate in a much more roundabout way. Verb forms, for instance, may be differentiated according to whether the speaker is reporting a situation or expecting it, and according to an event's duration, intensity, or other characteristics. It would not be too surprising, therefore, if the world-view of a people whose language does not 'have tenses' were rather different from our own: their concept of time, and perhaps even of cause and effect, might be somewhat different.

A more detailed example will clarify this situation. Consider the following four English sentences:

1. *I see that it is new.*
2. *I see that it is red.*
3. *I hear that it is new.*
4. *I hear that it is red.*

Each consists of two halves connected by the word *that*. In the American Indian language Hopi – one of the languages which led Whorf to formulate this hypothesis – the situation is very different.

The equivalent of sentence 1 in Hopi has one word for *that*, sentence 2 has another, and sentences 3 and 4 share yet another. Why is this so? Our native language, because it affects the way we think, may make the reason for the distinction in Hopi difficult for us to grasp. Our world-view, due to our native language, does not permit instant understanding of a distinction which any Hopi would make automatically. In fact, the three different Hopi words for *that* are used because three different types of 'presentation to consciousness' are involved. In sentence 1 the newness of the object in question is inferred by the speaker from a number of different visual clues and from his past experience. In sentence 2, on the other hand, the redness of the object is received in the speaker's consciousness as the direct result of a visual sense stimulus. The processes involved are different, and this difference is reflected in the language. Hopi speakers are in no doubt that such a difference exists, whereas the speakers of European languages have to have it explained to them, or else take some time to work out a solution for themselves. In 3 and 4 the presentation to consciousness is different again: the redness and newness are both perceived as the result of a direct aural stimulus. In this case, however, both characteristics are established in exactly the same way, and so only one relating word is involved.

The point of this example is to illustrate that in some cases differences of language may lead to differences in perception of the world. It suggests that the Hopi habitually perceives his environment in a rather different way from English speakers, who have some problems in appreciating the normal Hopi distinction. However, it is entirely possible for us to understand the distinction. Moreover, translation between Hopi and English is also a perfectly feasible exercise. This indicates that any strong form of the Sapir–Whorf hypothesis – say, that thought is actually constrained by language – cannot be accepted. The example may well be taken to indicate, however, that habitual thought is to a certain extent conditioned by language. English speakers are not normally aware of the different types of presentation to consciousness illustrated above – though constraints of this type can be overcome quite easily if necessary.

The Sapir–Whorf hypothesis is concerned with the possibility that man's view of his environment may be conditioned by his language. Less controversial is the one-way relationship that operates in the opposite direction – the effect of society on language, and the way in which environment is reflected in language. First, there are many examples of the *physical* environment in which a society lives being reflected in its language, normally in the structure of its lexicon – the way in which distinctions are made by means of single words. Whereas English, for example, has only one word for *snow* (or two if we include *sleet*), Eskimo has several. The reasons for this are obvious. It is essential for Eskimoes to be able to distinguish efficiently between different types of snow. English, of course, is quite able to make the same distinctions: *fine snow, dry snow, soft snow,* and so on, but in Eskimo this sort of distinction is lexicalized – made by means of individual words. In the same way the Lapp languages of northern Scandinavia have many words associated with reindeer, and Bedouin Arabic has a large camel vocabulary.

Secondly, the *social* environment can also be reflected in language, and can often have an effect on the structure of the vocabulary. For example, a society's kinship system is generally reflected in its kinship vocabulary, and this is one reason why anthropologists tend to be interested in this particular aspect of language. We can assume, for example, that the important kin relationships in English-speaking societies are those that are signalled by single vocabulary items; *son, daughter, grandson, granddaughter, brother, sister, father, mother, husband, wife, grandfather, grandmother, uncle, aunt, cousin.* We can, of course, talk of other relationships such as *eldest son, maternal aunt, great uncle,* and *second cousin,* – but the distinction between 'maternal' and 'paternal' aunt is not important in our society, and is not reflected in the English lexicon.

This point can be amplified by reference to the kinship vocabularies of other communities. In the Australian aboriginal language Njamal, for example, there are, as in English, fifteen lexicalized kinship distinctions, but the way in which these terms compare with their English equivalents reveals much about the differences between the two societies. The Njamal term *mama* signifies what for the Njamal is a single kinship relationship, but which has to be translated into English in different ways according to context: *father, uncle, male cousin of parent,* and so on. In other words, the term is used for all males of the same generation as the father. For the English speaker, the most striking fact is that the two English words *father* and *uncle* can be translated by one Njamal term. Clearly the distinction between *father* and *father's brother* cannot have the same importance in Njamal society as in our own. On the other hand, whereas English employs the term *uncle* for *father's brother* and *mother's sister's husband,* as well as for *mother's brother* and *father's sister's husband,* Njamal uses *mama* for the first pair and another term, *karna,* for the second. Other Njamal kinship terms distinguish not generation, as in English, but generation distance. For example, a man can use the same term, *maili,* for his *father's father* and his *daughter's son's wife's sister,* the point being that the person in question is two generations removed.

As society is reflected in language in this way, social change can produce a corresponding linguistic change. If, for example, the structure of Njamal society altered radically so that it came to resemble more closely that of English-speaking Australians, we would expect the linguistic system to alter correspondingly. This has happened in the case of Russian. During the period from 1860 to the present day the structure of the Russian kinship system has undergone a very radical change as a result of several important events: the emancipation of serfs in 1861, the First World War, the revolution, the collectivization of agriculture and the Second World War. There has been a marked social as well as political revolution, and this has been accompanied by a corresponding change in the language. For example, in the middle of the last century, *wife's brother* was *shurin,* whereas now it is simply *brat zheny, brother of wife.* Similarly, *brother's wife,* formerly *nevestka,* is now *zhena brata, wife of brother.* In other words, distinctions that were formerly lexicalized, because they were important, are now made by means of phrases. The loss of importance of these particular relationships, and the corresponding linguistic changes, are due to the fact that social changes in Russia have led to the rise of the small, nuclear family. In the last century most Russians lived in large patrilocal extended-family households. Brother's wives, at that time part of the family, now normally live in different households. Similarly, the term *yatrov*, signifying *husband's brother's wife* has now disappeared entirely. In earlier days it was a very important term, meaning for the women who used it a person of the same status as herself – a woman from outside married into the father-centred household. As the significance of this status has been lost (not the relationship itself, of course), so has the relevant vocabulary item.

And it is not only kinship terms which may reflect the structure of society. In English, as in several other languages, one of the normal ways of pronominalizing nouns like *person* for which sex is not specified is by the pronoun *he*, not *she*. Phrases like *the first person to finish his dinner* can refer to people of both sexes, but *the first person to finish her dinner* could refer only to females. Similarly, we can talk about *a speaker's use of his language* without implying that only male speakers are involved. The fact that *he* can be used in this way and that *she* cannot may well reflect the traditionally male-dominated structure of our society. (The more colloquial form, *the first person to finish* their *dinner*, may also perhaps reflect a partial breakdown in this dominance pattern.)

Thirdly, in addition to environment and social structure, the *values* of a society can also have an effect on its language. The most interesting way in which this happens is through the phenomenon known as *taboo*. Taboo can be characterized as being concerned with behaviour which is believed to be supernaturally forbidden, or regarded as immoral or improper; it deals with behaviour which is prohibited or inhibited in an apparently irrational manner. In language, taboo is associated with things which are *not* said, and in particular with words and expressions which are *not* used. In practice, of course, this simply means that there are inhibitions about the normal use of items of this kind – if they were not said at all they could hardly remain in the language.

Taboo words occur in most languages, and failure to adhere to the often strict rules governing their use can lead to punishment or public shame. Many people will never employ words of this type, and most others will only use them in a restricted set of situations. For those who do use taboo words, however, 'breaking the rules' may have connotations of strength or freedom which they find desirable.

Generally, the type of word that is tabooed in a particular language will be a good reflection of at least part of the system of values and beliefs of the society in question. In some communities, word-magic plays an important part in religion, and certain words regarded as powerful will be used in spells and incantations. In different parts of the world taboo words include those for the left hand, for female relations, or for certain game animals. Some words, too, are much more severely tabooed than others. In the English-speaking world, the most severe taboos are now associated with words connected with sex, closely followed by those connected with excretion and the Christian religion. This is a reflection of the great emphasis traditionally placed on sexual morality in our culture. In other, particularly Roman Catholic, cultures the strongest taboos may be associated with religion, and in Norway, for example, some of the most strongly tabooed expressions are concerned with the devil.

Until recently, the strict rules associated with some taboo words in English received legal as well as social reinforcement. Not so long ago, the use in print of words such as *fuck* and *cunt* could lead to prosecution and even imprisonment, and they are still not widely used in newspapers. Laws of this type have been relaxed in Britain and America, but there are still some parts of the English-speaking world where this is not the case. It may be unwise even now to use such words in public in Britain, although at least one magistrate has ruled that *fuck* is no longer obscene, i.e. legally tabooed.

There is, of course, a certain amount of 'double-think' about words of this type. Although their use was, and may still be, technically illegal in some cases, they occur very frequently in the speech of some sections of the community. This is largely because taboo-words are frequently used as swear-words, which is in turn because they are *powerful*. Most people in modern technologically advanced societies would claim not to believe in magic. There is still, however, something that very closely resembles magic surrounding the use of taboo-words in English. The use of taboo-words in non-permitted contexts, such as on television, provokes violent reactions of apparently very real shock and disgust. The reaction, moreover, is an irrational reaction to a particular word, not to a concept. It is perfectly permissible to say 'sexual intercourse' on television. Taboo is therefore clearly a linguistic as well as sociological fact. It is the words themselves which are felt to be wrong and are therefore so powerful.

The strength of this magic is illustrated by the way in which the BBC has on some occasions gone to considerable technical lengths to ensure that telephoned contributions from the public to certain radio programmes broadcast live could be cut off if they contained taboo words. One can infer that they were worried or perhaps even frightened by the prospect of the use of certain words – or the effects of their use. It has also been suggested that one reason for the general exclusion of uneducated people from widespread participation in broadcast programmes is the fear that they will not 'know the rules' about taboo. Taboo-words may be in order in certain situations, but they are not yet generally acceptable on television.

The phrase 'not yet' indicates the rapidity with which patterns of taboo in English are changing. Legal sanctions are disappearing and there is a growing tendency for more rational, less magical attitudes to develop towards taboo – 'breaking the rules' is now less dramatic than it used to be, at least in certain situations. (A well-known example of this is Shaw's use of *bloody*, now relatively harmless, as a shock-word in *Pygmalion*. Here, too, social change is reflected in a change in linguistic behaviour.)

A further interesting point is the secondary effect that taboo can have on language itself. Because of the strong reluctance of speakers to utter taboo-words, or words like them, in certain circumstances, words which are phonetically similar to taboo-words can be lost from a language. It is often said, for example, that *rabbit* replaced the older word *coney* (pronounced [kʌni]) in English for this reason. A similar explanation is advanced for the widespread American use of *rooster* rather than *cock*. In the case of bilingual individuals, this can even take place across languages, apparently. American Indian girl speakers of Nootka have been reported by teachers to be entirely unwilling to use the English word *such* because of the close phonetic resemblance it bears to the Nootka word for *vagina*. Similarly, Thai students in England are said to avoid the use of Thai words such as [khaɪn] 'to crush' when speaking Thai in the presence of English speakers, in the belief that this could cause offence.

These, then, are some of the ways in which society acts upon language and, possibly, in which language acts upon society. We have seen that there are a number of ways in which language and society are inter-related, and in the following chapters we shall investigate some further aspects of this kind of inter-relationship. In the past ten or fifteen years, increasing recognition of the importance of this relationship has led to the growth of a relatively new sub-discipline within linguistics: *sociolinguistics*. It is a broad but fair generalization to say that much of linguistics has in the past completely ignored the relationship between language and society. In most cases this has been for very good reasons. Concentration on the 'idiolect' – the speech of one person at one time in one style – was a necessary simplification that led to several theoretical advances. However, as we have already indicated, language is very much a social phenomenon. A study of language totally without reference to its social context inevitably leads to the omission of some of the more complex and interesting aspects of language and to the loss of opportunities for further theoretical progress. One of the main factors that has led to the growth of sociolinguistic research has been the recognition of the importance of the fact that language is a very variable phenomenon, and that this variability may have as much to do with society as with language. A language is not a simple, single code used in the same manner by all people in all situations, and linguistics has now arrived at a stage where it is both possible and beneficial to begin to tackle this complexity.

Sociolinguistics, then, is that part of linguistics which is concerned with language as a social and cultural phenomenon. It makes use of the subject matter, methodology or findings of the social sciences – sociology and social anthropology in the main, but it also impinges in certain respects on social or human geography. In this way it is possible to talk of *sociological*, *anthropological* and *geographical* linguistics, according to which of the three social sciences is most closely involved. The work mentioned above on the English spoken in New York (see p. 22) is an example of sociological linguistics, since it was a large-scale study of an industrialized urban community using a number of techniques developed by sociologists. The study of Njamal kinship terms, on the other hand, is a good example of anthropological linguistics. The study of the way in which dialects vary gradually from one region to another, as from Norfolk to Suffolk, or Holland to Germany, comes under geographical linguistics, as do a number of the topics we shall be discussing in Chapter 7. (Much of geographical linguistics, however, is covered by the heading, traditional in linguistics, of *linguistic geography*, which in turn is part of *dialectology*. Dialectology, although it is involved with the interaction of language and society, is a much older subject than sociolinguistics. It has a considerable body of literature of its own, as well as a number of distinct methods and traditions.) Finally, at some points in our study of sociolinguistics we shall be concerned with what can perhaps be termed 'sociolinguistics proper'. This covers studies of language in its social context which (whether they be sociological, anthropological or geographical in emphasis) are mainly concerned with answering questions of interest to linguists, such as how can we improve our theories about the nature of language, and how and why does language change. We have already mentioned certain insights into linguistic change obtained from the New England and New York studies. At other points, especially in Chapter 6, 'Language and Nation', we shall be dealing with topics which come more appropriately under the heading 'the sociology of language'. This is more specifically concerned with how, when and why people in different communities use language varieties, and with social, political and educational aspects of the relationship between language and society.

2. Language and Social Class

If you are an English-speaker you will be able to estimate the relative social status of the following speakers solely on the basis of the linguistic evidence given here:

Speaker A	Speaker B
I done it yesterday.	*I did it yesterday.*
He ain't got it.	*He hasn't got it.*
It was her what said it.	*It was her that said it.*

If you heard these speakers say these things you would guess that B was of higher social status than A, and you would almost certainly be right. How is it that we are able to do this sort of thing?

The answer lies in the existence of varieties of language which have come to be called *social-class dialects*. There are grammatical differences between the speech of these two speakers which give us clues about their social backgrounds. It is also probable, although this is not indicated on the printed page, that these differences will be accompanied by phonetic and phonological differences – that is to say, there are also different *social-class accents*. The internal differentiation of human societies is reflected in their languages. Different social groups use different linguistic varieties, and as experienced members of a speech community we (and our man in the railway compartment) have learnt to classify speakers accordingly. Why does social differentiation have this effect on language? We may note parallels between the development of these social varieties and the development of regional varieties: in both cases *barriers* and *distance* appear to be relevant. Dialectologists have found that regional-dialect boundaries often coincide with *geographical* barriers, such as mountains, swamps or rivers: for example, all local-dialect speakers in the areas of Britain north of the river Humber (between Lincolnshire and Yorkshire) still have a monophthong in words like *house* ('*hoose*' [huːs]), whereas speakers south of the river have had some kind of [haus]-type diphthong for several hundred years. It also seems to be the case that the greater the geographical distance between two dialects the more dissimilar they are linguistically: for instance, those regional varieties of British English which are most unlike the speech of London are undoubtedly those of the north-east of Scotland – Buchan, for example. The development of social varieties can perhaps be explained in the same sort of way – in terms of *social* barriers and *social* distance. The diffusion of a linguistic feature through a society may be halted by barriers of social class, age, race, religion or other factors. And social distance may have the same sort of effect as geographical distance: a linguistic innovation that begins amongst, say, the highest social group will affect the lowest social group last, if at all. (We must be careful, however, not to explain all social differences of language in these entirely mechanical terms since, as we saw in Chapter 1, *attitudes* to language clearly play an important role in preserving or removing dialect differences.)

Of the many forms of social differentiation, for example by class, age, sex, race or religion, we shall concentrate in this chapter on the particular type of social differentiation illustrated in the example of speakers A and B – *social stratification*. Social stratification is a term used to refer to any hierarchical ordering of groups within a society. In the industrialized societies of the West this takes the form of stratification into social classes, and gives rise linguistically to social-class dialects. (The whole question of social class is in fact somewhat controversial, especially since sociologists are not agreed as to the exact nature, definition or existence of social classes. There is little point, however, in attempting to list or evaluate here the different approaches adopted by sociological theorists to this topic. Suffice it to say that social classes are generally taken to be aggregates of individuals with similar social and/or economic characteristics. The general attitude adopted towards social class in most linguistic studies will emerge from the following paragraphs.) Social-class stratification is not universal, however. In India, for example, society is stratified into different *castes*. As far as the linguist is concerned, *caste dialects* are in some ways easier to study and describe than social-class dialects. This is because castes are stable, clearly named groups, rigidly separated from each other, with hereditary membership and with little possibility of movement from one caste to another. (This is a considerable simplification of the actual situation, but my main point is to emphasize the difference between caste and class societies.) Because of this rigid separation into distinct groups, caste-dialect differences tend to be relatively clear-cut and social differences in language are sometimes greater than regional differences. Table 2 illustrates

Table 2. Regional and caste differences in Kanarese

| | Brahmin | | non-Brahmin | |
	Dharwar	Bangalore	Dharwar	Bangalore
'it is'	ǝdǝ	ide	ayti	ayti
'inside'	-oḷage	-alli	-āga	-āga
infinitive affix	-likke	-ōk	-āk	-āk
participle affix	-ō	-ō	-ā	-ā
'sit'	kūt-	kūt-	kunt-	kunt-
reflexive	kō	kō	kont-	kont-

these points with data from Kanarese, a Dravidian language of south India. It shows a number of forms used by Brahmins, the highest caste, and their equivalents in the speech of the lower castes, in two towns, Bangalore and Dharwar, which are about 250 miles apart.

The first three examples show that, although the Bangalore and Dharwar forms are the same for the lower castes, the Brahmin caste has forms which are not only different from the other castes but also *different from each other* in the two towns. The higher-caste forms are more localized than the lower-caste forms. (We shall see that the reverse is true of class varieties of English.) The second three examples show that there is more similarity within social than geographical groups – social distance is more differentiating than geographical distance.

In the class societies of the English-speaking world the social situation is much more fluid, and the linguistic situation is therefore rather more complex, at least in certain respects. Social classes are not clearly defined or labelled entities but simply aggregates of people with similar social and economic characteristics; and social mobility – movement up or down the social hierarchy – is perfectly possible. This makes things much more difficult for any linguist who wishes to describe a particular variety – the more heterogeneous a society is, the more heterogeneous is its language. For many years the linguist's reaction to this complexity was generally to ignore it – in two rather different ways. Many linguists concentrated their studies on the *idiolect* – the speech of one person at one time in one style – which was thought (largely erroneously, as it happens – see p. 39) to be more regular than the speech of the community as a whole. Dialectologists, on the other hand, concentrated on the speech of rural informants, and in particular on that of elderly people of little education or travel experience, in small isolated villages. Even small villages are socially heterogeneous, of course, but it is easier to ignore this fact in villages than in large towns. It is only fair to say, however, that there are two additional explanations for why dialectologists concentrated on rural areas in this way. First, they were concerned to record many dialect features which were dying out before they were lost for ever. Secondly, there was a feeling that hidden somewhere in the speech of older, uneducated people were the 'real' or 'pure' dialects which were steadily being corrupted by the standard variety, but which the dialectologist could discover and describe if he was clever enough. (It turns out that the 'pure' homogeneous dialect is also largely a mythical concept: all language is subject to stylistic and social differentiation, because all human communities are functionally differentiated and heterogeneous to varying degrees. All language varieties are also subject to change. There is, therefore, an element of differentiation even in the most isolated conservative rural dialect.) Gradually, however, dialectologists realized that by investigating only the speech of older, uneducated speakers they were obtaining an imperfect and inaccurate picture of the speech of different areas. (For example, the records of the

Survey of English Dialects show that Surrey is an area where postvocalic /r/ is pronounced in words like *yard* and *farm* (see p. 158) whereas anybody who has been to Surrey will know that this is simply not the case for the majority of the population.)

Dialectologists then began to incorporate social as well as geographical information into their dialect surveys. For example, workers on the Linguistic Atlas of the United States and Canada, which was begun in the 1930s, divided their informants into three categories largely according to the education they had received, and thereby added a social dimension to their linguistic information. They also began, in a rather tentative kind of way, to investigate the speech of urban areas. It was not really until after the Second World War, however, that linguists also began to realize that in confining dialect studies to mainly rural areas they were remaining singularly ignorant about the speech of the vast majority of the population – those who lived in towns. A large amount of linguistic data that was both interesting in itself and potentially valuable to linguistic theory was being ignored or lost. For this reason, works with titles like *The Speech of New York City* and *The Pronunciation of English in San Francisco* now began to appear. Urban studies presented a further problem, however – how on earth could a linguist describe 'the speech of New York City' – a city of eight million or more inhabitants? How accurate was it to refer to the 'English in San Francisco' when your work was based on the analysis of the speech of only a small number of the tens of thousands of speakers you could have investigated? Was it, in other words, legitimate or worthwhile to apply the methods of traditional rural dialectology to large urban areas? The answer was eventually seen to be 'No'.

Those urban dialectologists who recognized that this was the case were therefore forced to work out how they were to describe, *fully* and *accurately*, the speech of large towns and cities, and it was in response to this problem that urban dialectology eventually became sociolinguistic (sociological linguistic, in fact). In 1966, the American linguist, William Labov, published in *The Social Stratification of English in New York City* the results of a large-scale survey of the speech of New York. He had carried out tape-recorded interviews, not with a handful of informants, but with 340. Even more important, his informants were selected, not through friends or personal contacts (as had often been the case earlier), but by means of a scientifically designed random sample, which meant that though not everybody could be interviewed, everybody had an equal *chance* of selection for interview. By bringing sociological methods such as random sampling to linguistics, Labov was able to claim that the speech of his informants was truly representative of that of New York (or at least of the particular area he investigated, the Lower East Side). Since the informants were a representative sample, the linguistic description could therefore be an *accurate* description of *all* the varieties of English spoken in this area. Labov also developed techniques, later refined, for eliciting normal speech from people in spite of the presence of the tape-recorder. (This was an important development which we shall discuss further in Chapter 5.) He also developed methods for the quantitative measurements of linguistic data which will be described in part below. Since this breakthrough other studies of urban dialects have been and are being made, on both sides of the Atlantic, on the same sort of pattern.

The methods developed by Labov have proved to be very significant for the study of social-class dialects and accents. The methods of traditional dialectology may be adequate for the description of caste dialects (though even this is doubtful) since any individual, however selected, stands a fair chance of being not too different from the caste group as a whole. But it is not possible to select any single speaker and to generalize from him to the rest of the speakers in his social-class group. This was an important point that was demonstrated by Labov. The speech of a single speaker (his idiolect) may differ considerably from those of others like him. Moreover, it may also be internally very inconsistent. The speech of most New Yorkers appeared to vary in a completely random and unpredictable manner. Sometimes they would say *guard* with an /r/, sometimes without. Sometimes they would say *beard* and *bad* in the same way, sometimes they would make a difference. Linguists have traditionally called this 'free variation'.

Labov showed, however, that the variation is not free. Viewed against the background of the speech community as a whole the variation was not random but determined by extra-linguistic factors in a quite predictable way. That is, the researcher could not predict on any one occasion whether an individual would say *cah* or *car*, but he could show that, if he was of a certain social class, age and sex, he would use one or other variant approximately *x* per cent of the time, on average, in a given situation. The idiolect might appear random, but the speech community was quite predictable. In any case, by means of methods of the type employed by Labov the problem of the heterogeneity of speech communities has been, at least partly, overcome. We are now able to correlate linguistic features with social class accurately, and obtain thereby a clearer picture of social dialect differentiation.

As far as English is concerned, linguists have known for a long time that different dialects and accents are related to differences of social-class background. In Britain, we can describe the situation today in the following, somewhat simplified way. Conservative, and, in particular, rural dialects – old-fashioned varieties associated with groups lowest in the social hierarchy – change gradually as one moves across the countryside. The point made in Chapter 1 about travelling from Norfolk into Suffolk is equally valid for a journey from Cornwall to Aberdeen: there exists a whole series of different dialects which gradually merge into one another. This series is referred to as a *dialect continuum* – a large number of different but not usually distinct non-standard dialects connected by a chain of similarity, but with the dialects at either end of the chain being very dissimilar. At the other end of the social scale, however, the situation is very different. Speakers of the highest social class employ the dialect we have called standard English, which, as we saw in Chapter 1, is only very slightly different in different parts of the country. The situation can therefore be portrayed as in Figure 1. To take a lexical example, there is in the standard English dialect a single word *scarecrow* signifying the humanoid object farmers place in fields to scare off birds. At the other end of the pyramid, on the other hand, we find a far greater degree of regional variation in

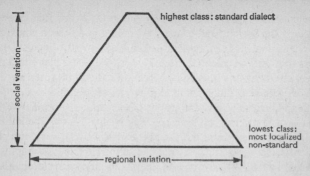

Figure 1. Social and regional dialect variation

the most localized regional English dialects. Corresponding to *scarecrow* we have *bogle, flay-crow, mawpin, mawkin, bird-scarer, moggy, shay, guy, bogeyman, shuft, rook-scarer*, and several others. The same sort of pattern is also found with grammatical differences. In standard English, for example, we find both:

> *He's a man who likes his beer.*   and
> *He's a man that likes his beer.*

But regional variation in non-standard varieties is much greater. All the following are possible:

> *He's a man who likes his beer.*
> *He's a man that likes his beer.*
> *He's a man at likes his beer.*
> *He's a man as likes his beer.*
> *He's a man what likes his beer.*
> *He's a man he likes his beer.*
> *He's a man likes his beer.*

As far as accent is concerned, the situation is slightly different, as portrayed in Figure 2, because of the unique position of RP. (This is not to say that there is no variation within RP, but what there is is generally not regionally determined.) This means that

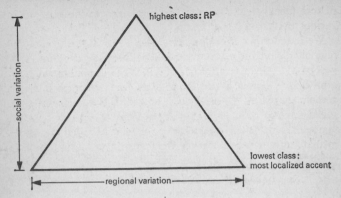

Figure 2. Social and regional accent variation

at any given point in England, and at least in parts of the rest of the United Kingdom, there is a continuum of accents ranging from RP, through various local accents, to the most localized accent associated with the lowest social class. Table 3 illustrates

Table 3. RP and local-accent pronunciation of home

	Edin-burgh	New-castle	Liver-pool	Bradford	Dudley	Norwich	London
RP	həʊm	həʊm	həʊm	həʊm	həʊm	həʊm	həʊm
Inter-mediate	hoːm	hoːm	hoʊm	hoʊm	hɔʊm	huːm	hʌʊm
	hoːm	huom	hoːm	hɔːm	ɔʊm	hʊm	ʌʊm
Most localized	heːm	hiem jem	oːm	ɔːm	wʊm	ʊm	æʊm

this situation as it affects the pronunciation of one word, *home*. In the top line of this table there is only one variant, while there are seven on the bottom line. In the second line, moreover, the presence of [hoːm] in both Edinburgh and Newcastle, and, particularly, of [hoʊm] in both Liverpool and Bradford, indicates the way in which certain non-RP pronunciations acquire the status of less locally restricted, regional standard pronunciations in various parts of the country.

We have known for a long time about this kind of social and regional dialect and accent variation, and we have also been fairly well provided with descriptions of RP. We have not known, however, exactly how RP and the intermediate and most localized accents are related to social class; how far RP extends down the social scale in different places; what kind of speaker uses the regional standard pronunciation; and exactly what the intermediate and localized accents are like. Linguists are now in a position to begin to answer these questions.

If we are to obtain a correct picture of the relationship between language and social stratification we must be able to *measure* both linguistic and social phenomena so that we can correlate the two accurately. As far as social class is concerned this can be done relatively easily (it is still far from simple) by the sociological method of assigning an individual a numerical index score on the basis of his occupational, income, educational and/or other characteristics, and then grouping him together with others with similar indexes (although the justification for different groupings may be controversial). Measuring language is more difficult. The solution developed by Labov and since used by others is to take linguistic features which are known, either from previous study or intuitively by the linguist as a native speaker, to vary within the community being studied, and which are also easily countable in some way. For instance, in two separate surveys, one in Detroit, USA, and one in Norwich, England, the same grammatical feature appeared to be suitable in this way. In standard English the third-person present-tense singular form of verbs has an affix, orthographic -*s*, which distinguishes it from other persons: *I know, we know, they know,* but *she knows.* In East Anglia and in Detroit this -*s* is often not present, at least in the speech of some people. This means that the following sorts of form occur:

> *She like him very much.*
> *He don't know a lot, do he?*
> *It go ever so fast.*

Since standard English has the -*s*, and since the standard variety is generally most closely associated with higher social groups, it was suspected that there might be a direct correlation between social class position and usage of -*s*. To investigate this possibility was relatively easy, since there was no difficulty in measuring this linguistic feature: it was simply a matter of listening to tape-recordings made during the surveys and counting the number of times a speaker did or did not use -*s*. Table 4 shows the results of

Table 4. Verbs without -s in Norwich and Detroit

	Norwich		Detroit
MMC	0%	UMC	1%
LMC	2	LMC	10
UWC	70	UWC	57
MWC	87	LWC	71
LWC	97		

these investigations for Norwich speakers and for Negro speakers in Detroit. The table shows that the suspicion is quite justified – there is a clear correlation between social class and usage of -*s*. (Norwich informants have been divided into five social-class groups – middle middle class; lower middle class; upper working class; middle working class; and lower working class – on the basis of their social-class index scores. The linguists working with the Detroit informants divided them into four social-class groups.)

The relationship is obvious – but what exactly is the value of this kind of information? First, it shows precisely what sort of information we are working with when we assign a social status to a speaker on the basis of linguistic evidence. Through our linguistic experiences we have become sensitive, normally subconsciously, to correlations of this type between social class and standard or local linguistic forms. Secondly, it tells us a little about the social structure of the two communities. In both cases, by far the biggest gap between any two scores is that between the LMC and the UWC. This suggests that the division of society into two main class groups, 'middle class' and 'working class', a division made largely but not entirely on the basis of the difference between manual and non-manual occupations, is of some validity and importance, since the social barrier is clearly reflected in language. Thirdly, it illustrates the point made above about the idiolect. Although individuals will sometimes use one verb form, and sometimes another, the average percentage for each group falls into a quite predictable pattern.

Finally, it tells us a lot about social-class dialects. Even though we are concentrating on only one feature rather than on a variety as a whole, it is still apparent that, like regional dialects, social-class dialects are not distinct entities. They merge into each other to form a continuum. We can if we like talk of 'the middle-working-class Norwich dialect', but if we do we must be very clear (a) that our division into five social classes may be arbitrary; (b) that the linguistic differences involved are simply relative and involve the frequency of occurrence of particular features; and (c) there may be differing results if other linguistic variables are taken. Popular stereotypes of social-class dialects are therefore almost always misleading: it is not accurate, for example, to make statements like, 'The Detroit Negro dialect has no third-person marker on present-tense verbs.' Detroit Negroes of all social classes use forms both of the *it go* and of the *it goes* type – it is only the proportions which are different.

Now, the situation portrayed in both the above cases could be regarded as being a case of *dialect mixture*. We could say, that is, that in the first case what we are *really* faced with is two different dialects, one with and one without the *-s*. (The Norwich MMC score gives some support to this view.) We could then state that these two separate dialects are mixed in different proportions by speakers from different classes. This may in fact be a valid historical explanation of how this situation arose in the first place. In my view, however, (and not all linguists would agree with me) it is better to describe the present-day situation as a case of *inherent variability* (at least in Norwich – the position in Detroit is less clear). *Inherent variability* means that the variation is due not to the mixture of two or more varieties but is an integral part of the variety itself. Thus according to the 'dialect-mixture view' Detroit Negro speakers vary their verb forms because they mix Detroit Negro English (which in its 'pure' form does not have -*s*) with standard English (which does). According to the 'inherent-variability view', on the other hand, this variation is simply one characteristic of Detroit Negro English. The evidence for this second view is that this kind of variation takes place on a very wide scale, involving all speakers and a very large number of other linguistic features. More tellingly, this kind of variability is found even in the speech of very young children who have not been exposed to other dialects. Linguistic varieties, at least in urban areas, appear to be inherently variable as a rule rather than as an exception, and inherent variability is probably the linguistic counterpart of social heterogeneity.

A number of other, rather more complex grammatical features have also been shown to correlate with social class in the same kind of patterned manner – to characterize, by their frequency of occurrence, different (but non-discrete) class dialects. Consider, for example, what happens if we wish to negate the following sentence:

I can eat anything.

There are two possibilities in the standard variety of English. We can either negate the verb, to produce:

I can't eat anything.

or we can negate the pronoun:

I can eat nothing.

(The same is true of other similar sentences containing an indefinite article or pronoun.) There are other varieties of English, however, where there is a third possibility – where we can negate both elements:

I can't eat nothing.

It was found in the Detroit survey that there was a clear relationship, again of the relative-frequency type, between employment of the third possibility, double negation, and social class. The percentages of non-standard forms used were:

UMC 2
LMC 11
UWC 38
LWC 70

– again we have the same sort of class pattern, and again no single class consistently uses only one form or the other.

Social-class *accents*, in contrast to grammatical features, appear rather more difficult to handle. We know, from our experience as native speakers, that there are a whole range of socially determined accents, but how exactly are we to correlate these phonetic and phonological features with sociological parameters? One problem is that many important class differences are signalled by prosodic features such as intonation, or by paralinguistic features like voice quality. The working-class accents of Birmingham, Liverpool and Norwich, for example, all have voice-quality features which distinguish them from their middle-class counterparts. (Birmingham and Liverpool speech is velarized, as are some types of New York speech, and Norwich speech is characterized by 'raised larynx voice'.) Unfortunately, techniques have not yet been developed for measuring this kind of differentiation, (although some attempts have been made to study the intonation of Newcastle English). On the other hand, it has been possible to investigate, singly, the pronunciation of individual vowels and consonants. It is, for example, relatively simple to count the presence or absence of particular consonants in any stretch of speech. In Norwich the following three features were studied:

1. the percentage of *n'* as opposed to *ng* in *walking, running*, etc. – [wɔːkn̩] versus [wɔːkɪŋ].
2. the percentage of glottal stops as opposed to *t* in *butter, bet*, etc. – [bʌʔə] versus [bʌtə].
3. the percentage of 'dropped *hs*' as opposed to *h* in *hammer, hat*, etc. – [æmə] versus [hæmə].

Table 5. Non-RP forms for three consonants in Norwich

	1. *ng*	2. *t*	3. *h*
MMC	31%	41%	6%
LMC	42	62	14
UWC	87	89	40
MWC	95	92	59
LWC	100	94	61

The results are shown in Table 5. The three consonants are clearly good indicators of social-class position in Norwich, and are particularly significant as indicators of membership of the middle-class or working-class as a whole. Once again, moreover, it seems that it is not possible to talk legitimately of discrete social-class accents – again there is a continuum, with most speakers using sometimes one pronunciation, sometimes another. (This means, of course, that Table 3 on p. 42 is a rather crude representation of the facts.) The vast majority of Norwich speakers use both pronunciations of all three consonants. It is also particularly interesting to note that even the highest class uses *walkin'*-type pronunciations 31 per cent of the time, on average.

Probably the first study of consonantal variation of this kind was made by Labov in New York City, prior to his main survey. The hypothesis that postvocalic /r/ usage would be correlated with social class was tested in an experiment rather more amusing than many linguistic investigations – by examining the speech of shop assistants in three different department stores, of high, medium and low status respectively. The procedure was to find out which departments were on the fourth floor and then to ask as many assistants as possible in the rest of the shop a question like, 'Excuse me, where are the women's shoes?' The answer to this would be *fourth floor* – with two possible occurrences of post-vocalic /r/. In this way information on /r/-usage was obtained from 264 informants (who did not know, of course, that they were being interviewed by a linguist). The results were: 38 per cent of the high-ranking store assistants used no /r/, 49 per cent in the middle store and 83 per cent in the low-ranking store. Thus, as well as acquiring a vast amount of rather restricted knowledge about the topography of New York City department stores, the investigator obtained an important indication of how socially significant a relatively trivial feature of accent can be.

With vowels, which are often socially more significant than consonants, the problem of measurement is greater, since it is not the presence or absence of a particular sound which is involved, but small (often very small) differences of vowel quality. (For example, it is often possible to tell whether RP speakers have been to a major public school or only to a minor one: the former tend to pronounce words such as *food* [fuːd], while the latter say [fuːd], i.e. the vowel is more front.) The linguist gets round this problem by distinguishing accurately (although often arbitrarily) between different vowel qualities and treating them as though they were discrete sounds. For example, there is a wide range of socially significant variation in New York English in the pronunciation of the vowel in *cab, bag, bad, half, path, dance*. The different variants form a continuum, but it is possible to split this up artificially, as in Table 6, into four distinct types. An

Table 6. New York vowels in bad

1. [bɪ°d]	cf. RP, NYC *beard*
2. [bɛˀd]	cf. RP, NYC *bared*
3. [bæd]	cf. North of England *bed*
4. [bæːd]	cf. RP, NYC *bad*

index score can then be calculated for each individual (and then for each class group) by calculating the average of the values assigned to each occurrence in his speech of this vowel. This will indicate the *average* pronunciation an individual or group uses – if an individual consistently says *bad, bag, half* as [bɪ°d] etc. he will score 1.0, whereas if he consistently says [bæːd] he will score 4.0. Results for three social-class groups were as follows:

UC 2.7
MC 2.5
LC 2.3

Thus, in casual conversation, all New Yorkers use on average a pronunciation between [bɛ°d] and [bæd], but there is a small but consistent difference between the social classes: lower-class speakers tend to use a closer vowel more frequently than higher-class speakers. A very small vowel-quality difference therefore turns out to be socially rather significant.

The same sort of technique has been used in the analysis of British accents. In Norwich English it is possible to distinguish three different vowel qualities in words such as *pass*, *part*, *shaft*, *bath*, *card*: 1. is the long back vowel [ɑː] of RP *pass* or New York *pot*, 2. is an intermediate vowel, and 3. is a front vowel [aː] similar to the vowel in Australian or eastern New England *part*. This means that scores can range from 1.0 for a consistent RP pronunciation to 3.0 for consistent use of the front vowel. The correlation of vowel quality with social class works out as follows:

MMC 1.9
LMC 2.1
UWC 2.8
MWC 2.9
LWC 3.0

Generally, WC speakers have a front vowel in Norwich English, while MC speakers have a central vowel, but there are still, on average, fine differences of vowel quality which distinguish one class from another. Many other class differences of the same kind could be cited from almost any area you care to name. In Leeds, for example, middle-class speakers tend to have a vowel of the [ʌ] type in words such as *but*, *up*, *fun*, while working-class speakers have a higher, rounder vowel, [ʊ]; in London, *name*, *gate*, *face* are pronounced [neɪm] etc., [nɛɪm], or [næɪm] depending on social class (highest-class form first); in Chicago the vowel of *roof*, *tooth*, *root* is most often [u] but is frequently more centralized [ʉ], in the speech of members of higher social-class groups; and in Boston, upper-class speakers have [ɵʊ] in *ago*, *know*, while other speakers have [oʊ].

This method of investigating social-class dialects and accents – measuring the social class of informants and then correlating linguistic data with that – has proved very useful. There is, however, another way of doing it. It is equally possible to group speakers together on the basis of their linguistic similarity, and then to see what, if any, social features characterize these groups. The technique of 'cluster analysis' is currently being employed in, amongst other cases, the analysis of Newcastle English, in an attempt to discover, by clustering speakers together on the basis of measures of linguistic similarity, what are the varieties of Newcastle English, and what are their social correlates. In many ways a technique of this kind appears to be equivalent to the method developed by Labov. It has an advantage over Labov's method in that social parameters of hitherto unsuspected importance may be revealed. On the other hand, it may be much more difficult to group speakers together on the basis of their linguistic rather than sociological characteristics.

In the final part of this chapter I want to consider a rather different aspect of the relationship between language and social class. It arises out of the work of Basil Bernstein, who is currently Professor in the Sociology of Education at the London University Institute of Education. Bernstein has postulated that there are two varieties of language available to speakers and has called these varieties 'elaborated code' and 'restricted code'. 'Elaborated code' tends to be used, according to Bernstein, in situations like a formal debate or academic discussion. It has the effect, Bernstein says, of imposing the speaker's individuality on the utterance (it stresses his unique nature as a person) and is context independent – that is, it does not rely on features of the extra-linguistic context (like facial expressions or a set of commonly shared assumptions) in order to convey its meaning. The 'elaborated code' is said to be characterized linguistically (although very few examples of any length have been given) by the use of a relatively high proportion of subordinate clauses, passive verbs, adjectives, uncommon adverbs and conjunctions, and the pronoun *I*. 'Restricted code', on the other hand, tends to be employed in informal situations, within the family or amongst friends, and it has the effect, Bernstein says, of stressing the speaker's membership of a group. It is generally tied to context in that a number of the shared assumptions of the group will be implicitly understood rather than overtly expressed, and there is relatively high predictability of which linguistic forms will be used. Linguistically 'restricted code' is signalled by a high proportion of personal pronouns, particularly *you* and *they*, by tag-questions soliciting the agreement of the listener, such as *wouldn't it?*, *aren't they?*, and so on, and by the absence of 'elaborated-code' features.

Now Bernstein has demonstrated, at least for some types of British English, that there is a relationship between the usage of these two 'codes' and social-class membership. It should be made clear, however, that there is no connection whatsoever between 'elaborated' and 'restricted code' on the one hand and social-class dialects on the other. This is made quite plain by the actual nature of the relationship Bernstein has demonstrated. In a number of experiments he has shown that, whereas middle-class children have access to (i.e. can and do use) both 'elaborated' *and* 'restricted code', *some* working-class children have access only to 'restricted code'. These findings have proved to be very influential in educational circles. A large amount of research has shown that working-class children do not do so well at school as middle-class children of the same intelligence. Bernstein's theory has been interpreted as providing a possible linguistic explanation for at least part of this phenomenon: although the educational situation demands the ability to use 'elaborated code', many working-class children do not use it.

If one accepts this point of view (and there are many who are unconvinced) then there are two possible positions one can adopt with respect to this problem, each resulting from the two different interpretations that can be put on the phrase 'the educational situation demands "elaborated code" '. *Position one* holds that it is simply *social convention* which requires a child to use 'elaborated code' in school. In other words, the demand is one made by society in general and teachers in particular. Teachers consider 'elaborated code' to be appropriate to the school situation, and children who do not use it may suffer educationally because they fail to live up to the teachers' expectations of what a bright or successful pupil should be like. If this is the case, then the situation

can be remedied by encouraging teachers not to base their evaluation of a child solely on his usage or non-usage of middle-class
speech patterns.

For *position two* the use of 'elaborated code' is *not* a social
convention but an essential requirement of the educational process itself. Certain educationalists, for example, have put forward
the view that working-class children do not have access to
'elaborated code' and that this leads to *cognitive deficiencies*. The
linguistic characteristics of 'restricted code', they say, produce
differences in working-class children's interpretation of the world,
or their ability to organize their experience, *vis-à-vis* middle-class
children. Since, moreover, the 'restricted code' is less 'adequate'
than 'elaborated code' to deal with certain concepts and modes
of thinking, this difference in world view means that working-
class children are cognitively (and hence educationally) deprived.
Because working-class children use relatively few abstract words,
for example, they are not able to handle abstract concepts: their
language is deficient.

This is a particularly strong statement of the 'language-deficit'
position, but one which is quite often advanced. Bernstein himself appears to adhere to a rather weaker version of this interpretation. He has specifically stated that, in his view, working-
class children are *not* linguistically deprived. But he does say that
the 'elaborated code' gives access to 'universalistic [i.e. context-
independent] orders of meaning' and that school 'is *necessarily*
concerned with the transmission and development of universalistic orders of meaning' (my emphasis). It is not therefore,
according to Bernstein, a matter of social convention. The
solution, according to this position, is to teach those children who
do not have access to 'elaborated code' to use it.

Criticisms of these positions have very recently been advanced.
First of all, let us deal with the less extreme version of position
two – the one adopted by Bernstein. It has been shown, to select
one of a number of possible criticisms, that working-class children
can produce 'elaborated code', particularly in writing. One can
infer that they do not *normally* produce 'elaborated code'
because they are not used to employing it in a particular situation,

or because they do not wish to. In part, Bernstein's original theory has now been modified to meet this criticism. First, Bernstein now believes that middle-class and working-class speakers may only differ in respect of the *contexts* which produce one code or another in their speech. Secondly, the two codes are not now seen as two discrete varieties, but simply indications of the different kinds of variants that can be used. Thirdly, it has been recognized that different types of family structure (which cut across class lines) are as important a differentiating factor as social class. Bernstein suggests that 'positional' families, where decision-making depends on the formal status of each member of the family as 'father', 'daughter', and so on, are less likely to give rise to 'the verbal elaboration of individual differences'. On the other hand, in families where judgements and decisions depend more on the member's individual personality than on his formal status – 'person-orientated' families – more 'open' communication systems are likely to arise.

In my own view, however, it is more important to argue against the strong version of position two, particularly since the 'language-deficit' view is now quite widely held. Its acceptance, moreover, has led to the development of several 'compensatory' educational programmes, particularly in the USA, which a number of linguists, at least, consider to be undesirable. Part of the impetus for these programmes has come from the work of Bernstein himself, although largely as a result of misinterpretations of his studies. The linguistic arguments against the 'language-deficit' view can be explained in the following way. As we saw in Chapter 1, some linguists have argued that difference of language can lead to difference in interpretation of the world. It is therefore not impossible that the linguistic differences, in so far as they have been enumerated, between the two 'codes' might give rise to cognitive differences (although we are very far from actually having any proof of this). However, there is no implication at all in any version of the Sapir–Whorf hypothesis that one language might produce a world view that is in any way superior to that produced by another: if there *are* differences, then they are merely differences. There is therefore no reason, in the absence of any evidence to the contrary, for introducing value judgements into a comparison of different 'codes' of the same language. There is also, furthermore, a certain amount of evidence *against* this position. Labov has provided an excellent example, now much quoted because so convincing, of the way in which working-class children can manipulate abstract concepts very skilfully even in 'restricted code'. A fifteen-year-old lower-class American Negro boy was asked by an interviewer to say, just for the sake of argument, if there was a God, what colour he would be:

INTERVIEWER: Jus' suppose there is a God, would he be white or black?

BOY: He'd be white, man.

INTERVIEWER: Why?

BOY: Why? I'll tell you why! Cause the average whitey out here got everything, you dig? And the nigger ain't got shit, y'know? Y'understan'? So - um - for in order for *that* to happen, you know it ain't no black God that's doin' that bullshit.

The argument he uses is not couched in standard English, nor does it have any of the characteristics of 'elaborated code'. It is nevertheless a complex argument, and one which represents a clear and effective use of language in which hypothetical cases and abstract concepts are handled competently. (This example underlines the value of the data obtained in urban language studies, and compares favourably with the widespread lack of illustrative data in papers dealing with 'restricted' and 'elaborated codes'.)

We can therefore suggest that the more extreme 'language-deficit' view incorporates a considerable element of *middle-class bias*. Middle-class speech is considered by some educationalists to be the desirable linguistic norm. If working-class children do not 'attain' this norm, then their language is considered to be defective. This view is justified by pointing to the child's relatively poor academic performance, which is in turn ascribed to the 'cognitive deprivation', due ultimately to 'linguistic deprivation'. Working-class language and bad academic record are causally linked in a manner which suggests that the fault lies with the language. The linguistic view, on the other hand, supported by Labov-type studies of language as it is actually used in everyday speech, is that working-class children are *not* 'linguistically deprived'. There are differences of social-class dialect, certainly, but as I have already stated, Bernstein is *not* dealing with a difference of this kind. We are therefore left with Bernstein's original discovery: middle-class children can or do use two different varieties of language, at least in some contexts, where working-class children use only one. What then *are* these varieties? I prefer to regard the linguistic differences that Bernstein has described as characteristic of the two 'codes' as being simply differences of *style*, within dialects, of the type we shall be dealing with in Chapter 5. We can then reinterpret Bernstein's findings as follows: in many contexts some working-class children are less willing or less used to employing a more formal style than are middle-class children. This, of course, by no means suggests that they are in any way linguistically deprived (particularly since stylistic variants are generally held to be equivalent ways of saying the same thing), although it may mean that working-class children have a narrower range of stylistic options open to them. (This, on the other hand, may well be compensated for by the fact that in many working-class groups verbal skills of particular types, such as joke-telling, narrating and insulting are very highly valued: there are probably certain options open to them which are not available to middle-class children.)

If, therefore, there is a linguistic explanation for the relatively poor school performance of working-class children it must be sought in the circumstances outlined under position one: more formal styles, although unnecessary, are *expected* in schools. But there is also a further factor: the variety of English used in school is standard English, whereas the language of working-class children, more so than middle-class children, is non-standard English. Educational difficulties can obviously result from this difference and will be discussed further in the next chapter.

3. Language and Ethnic Group

An experiment was carried out in the USA in which a number of people acting as judges were asked to listen to tape-recordings of two different sets of speakers. Many of the judges decided that speakers in the first set were black, and speakers in the second set white – and they were completely wrong, since it was the first set which consisted of white people, and the second of Negroes. But they were wrong in a very interesting way. The speakers they had been asked to listen to were exceptional people: the white speakers were people who had lived all their lives amongst blacks, or had been raised in areas where Negro cultural values were dominant; the black speakers were people who had been brought up, with little contact with other Negroes, in predominantly white areas. The fact was that the white speakers *sounded* like blacks, and the black speakers *sounded* like whites – and the judges listening to the tape-recordings reacted accordingly. This experiment demonstrates two rather important points. First, there are differences between the English spoken by many whites and many blacks in America such that Americans can, and do, assign people with some confidence to one of the two ethnic groups solely on the basis of their language – this might happen in a telephone conversation, for instance – which suggests that 'black speech' and 'white speech' have some kind of social reality for many Americans. This has been confirmed by other experiments, carried out in Detroit, which have shown that Detroiters of all ages and social classes have an approximately eighty per cent success rate in recognizing black or white speakers (from unexceptional backgrounds in this test) on the basis of only a few seconds of tape-recorded material. Secondly, the experiment demonstrates rather convincingly that, although the stereotypes of black or white speech which listeners work with provide them with a correct identification most of the time, the diagnostic differences are entirely the result of *learned* behaviour. People do not speak as they do *because* they are white or black. What does happen is that speakers acquire the linguistic characteristics of those they live in close contact with. Members of the two American ethnic groups we have been discussing learn the linguistic varieties associated with them in exactly the same way that social-class dialects are acquired, and in those unusual cases where whites live amongst blacks, or vice versa, the pattern acquired is that of the locally predominant group.

This means – and it may perhaps *still* be necessary to emphasize this – that there is no racial or physiological basis of any kind for linguistic differences of this type. In the past, of course, it was quite widely believed that there was or might be some connection between language and race. For example, during the nineteenth century, the originally linguistic term *Indo-European* came also to have racial connotations. The term *Indo-European* was coined to cover those languages of Europe, the Middle East, and India which, linguists had discovered, were historically related to each other. Subsequently, however, a myth grew up of an imaginary Indo-European or Aryan race who had not only spoken the parent Indo-European language but who were also the ancestors of the Germans, Romans, Slavs and of others who now speak Indo-European languages. Unfortunately for adherents of this view, any human being can learn any human language, and we know of many well-attested cases of whole ethnic groups switching language through time – one has only to think, for example, of the large numbers of people of African origin who now speak originally European languages. There can, therefore, be no guarantee whatsoever – indeed, it is exceptionally unlikely – that groups of people are 'racially related' because they speak related languages. We cannot say that Slavs and Germans are 'racially related' simply because they speak related Indo-European languages. Ideas about language and race die hard, however. The German language, for instance, was an important component of the Nazis' theories about the Germanic 'master race'; and false ideas about the possibility and desirability of preserving 'linguistic purity' (i.e. defending a language against 'contamination' by loan words from other languages) may often go hand in hand with equally false ideas about racial purity. (This is one of the reasons for the replacement of German words like *Geographie* by the supposedly purer *Erdkunde* during the Nazi period.) Perhaps less harmful, but probably much more persistent, are references to, for example, the Rumanians as a 'Latin' people (with all kinds of implications about 'national character') for no other reason than that they speak a Romance language. It is true, of course, that Rumanian represents a historical development of Latin (with a considerable admixture from Slavic and other languages), but it simply does not follow that Rumanians are genetically descendants of the Romans. It is, after all, much more likely that they are more closely related genetically to their Russian, Bulgarian and Hungarian neighbours, with whom they have been mixing for centuries, than to the 'Latin' Spaniards and Portuguese.

There is, then, no inherent or necessary link between language and race. It remains true, however, that in many cases language may be an important or even essential concomitant of ethnic-group membership. This is a social fact, though, and it is important to be clear about what sort of processes may be involved. In some cases, for example, and particularly where languages rather than varieties of a language are involved, linguistic characteristics may be the most important *defining* criteria for ethnic-group membership. For instance, it is less accurate to say that Greeks speak Greek than to state that people who are native speakers of Greek (i.e. who have Greek as their mother tongue) are generally considered to be Greek (at least by other Greeks) whatever their actual nationality. In other cases, particularly where different varieties of the same language are concerned, the connection between language and ethnic group may be a simple one of habitual association, reinforced by social barriers between the groups, where language is an important *identifying* characteristic. By no means all American Negroes speak 'Negro English', but the overwhelming majority of those who do speak it *are* Negroes, and can be identified as such from their speech alone. In these cases the connection, although not inevitable, is something members of the speech community come to expect, and the breaking of the connection may at first appear to result in incongruity: for this reason many people find it amusing to hear a white person with a West Indian accent or a black person with a Yorkshire accent. In any case, ethnic-group differentiation in a mixed community is a particular type of social differentiation and, as such, will often have linguistic differentiation associated with it.

Cases of the first type, where language is a *defining* characteristic of ethnic-group membership, are very common on a world scale. Situations of this type are very usual in multilingual Africa, for example. In one suburb outside Accra in Ghana there are native speakers of more than eighty different languages, including such major languages as Twi, Hausa, Ewe and Kru. In most cases, individuals will identify themselves as belonging to a particular ethnic group or tribe on the basis of which of these many languages is their mother tongue (although the majority of the inhabitants are bi- or tri-lingual). The different ethnic groups therefore maintain their separateness and identity as much through language as anything else. This is not only an African phenomenon, of course. The two main ethnic groups in Canada, for example, are distinguished mainly by language. For the most part, it is true, they also have different religions, different histories, cultures and traditions, but the most important defining characteristic is whether they are native speakers of English or French. Similarly, in American cities like Chicago there are groups of people who, although they are American citizens, may be identified as, say, 'German', 'Polish', 'Swedish' or 'Italian' by the language they speak (or used to speak) as well as or instead of English.

In cases of the second type – and these are in many ways more interesting – the separate identity of ethnic groups is signalled, not by different languages, but by different varieties of the same language. Differences of this type may originate in or at least be perpetuated by the same sorts of mechanisms as are involved in the maintenance of social-class dialects: we can suppose that ethnic group differentiation acts as a barrier to the communication of linguistic features in the same way as other social barriers. In the case of ethnic groups, moreover, attitudinal factors are likely to be of considerable importance. Individuals are much more likely to be aware of the fact that they are 'Jewish' or to consider themselves 'Negro' than they are to recognize that they are, say, 'lower middle class'. This means that ethnic-group membership may be an important social fact for them. Since, moreover, linguistic differences may be recognized, either consciously or subconsciously, as characteristic of such groups, these differences may be very persistent. An interesting example of this comes from Yugoslavia. Yugoslavia is a multilingual nation where language may act as a *defining* characteristic: Slovene, Macedonian, Albanian and Hungarian are spoken by ethnic groups ('nationalities' is the official Yugoslavian term) who go under the same name as the language. In other cases, however, different ethnic groups speak the same language, and here language may act as an *identifying* characteristic (although not, today, a particularly important one). This is true of Sarajevo, the capital of Bosnia, where the three main ethnic groups in the city, Serbs, Croats and Moslems, all speak Serbo-Croat, the most widely used Yugoslavian language. Historically speaking, this ethnic-group differentiation in Sarajevo has to do with religion (Serbs are or were Orthodox, Croats Catholic) and partly to do with geographical origin (Serbia is to the east of Bosnia, Croatia to the west). Today these factors are of no very great importance, but individuals are still aware of their ethnic group membership. Often, moreover, it is possible to detect ethnic background from linguistic clues. We cannot say, any more than we can with social-class dialects, that members of the three groups in Sarajevo speak distinct varieties. The differences are really only tendencies, and they appear to be entirely lexical: different words tend to be used more often by particular groups. The following list gives a few examples of the types of difference involved:

Moslems	Croats	Serbs	
hljeb	*kruh*	*hljeb*	'bread'
voz	*vlak*	*voz*	'train'
pendžer	*prozor*	*prozor*	'window'
čaršija	*grad*	*varoš*	'town'
sevdah	*ljubav*	*ljubav*	'love'
budžak	*kut*	*ćošak*	'corner'

It must be emphasized, too, that this list does not supply any hard and fast rules for usage by different groups, it merely gives indications of general trends. In most cases speakers from all three groups can and do use the other forms on occasions (except that Serbs and Croats are unlikely to use the Moslem words for *love* or *window*). The linguistic differences between the Serbs and Croats are largely geographical in origin in that the words they use tend to be those employed in Serbia and Croatia respectively. The typically Moslem words, on the other hand, tend to be loan words from Turkish, due to the influence of Islam and centuries of Turkish rule. In Sarajevo itself, however, these differences, whatever their origin, are today *ethnic-group* differences. They are perpetuated (in so far as they *are* maintained today) through members of each group associating more frequently with each other than with other groups, and perhaps more importantly, through the group-identification function that linguistic features often have.

In other cases of this sort, ethnic-group differences may be correlated with phonological or grammatical features, as well as or instead of with lexical differences. One of the interesting facts to emerge from Labov's New York study, for example, was that there were slight but apparently significant differences in the English pronunciation of speakers from Jewish, Italian and Negro backgrounds. These differences, once again, are statistical tendencies rather than clear-cut, reliable signals of ethnic-group difference, but they are clearly due to the fact that the different races tend to form separate groups within the city. In origin they appear to be due, at least to a certain extent, to the continuing effect of what are often called substratum varieties – the languages or varieties spoken by these groups or their forbears *before* they became speakers of New York City English – Yiddish, Italian and southern-states English. In the case of Yiddish and Italian the interference of the old language on the new (a 'Yiddish accent' in English, say) in the first generation has led to hyper-correction of foreign features by the second generation. For example, one of the characteristics of New York English, as we saw in the previous chapter (p. 49), has been the development of high *beard*-like vowels in words of the type *bad, bag*. It seems that this development has been accelerated by the desire, presumably subconscious, of second-generation Italians to avoid speaking English with an Italian accent. Native speakers of Italian tend to use an [a]-type vowel, more open than the English sound, in English words of this type, and their children, in wishing to avoid this pronunciation, may have selected the highest variants of this vowel available to them, i.e. the ones most unlike the typically Italian vowel. Certainly, Italians now show a notably greater tendency to use the higher vowels than do Jews, and this may eventually lead to a situation where high vowels in *bad, bag* become a symbol of identification for New Yorkers from Italian backgrounds. Jewish speakers, on the other hand, tend to have higher vowels than Italians in words of the type *off, lost, dog*, and a similar pattern of hypercorrection may be responsible for this: many native Yiddish speakers who have learnt English as a foreign language do not distinguish the /ɔ/ in *coffee* from the /ʌ/ in *cup*, so that *coffee cup* may be /kɔfi kɔp/. Second-generation speakers may therefore have exaggerated the difference between the two vowels, in order to stress the fact that they do make the distinction, with the result that higher vowels occur in *coffee, dog* [dʊ°g]. These high vowels are not the *result* of pressures of this sort, since high vowels are by no means confined to Jewish speakers, but they may well have been encouraged by this ethnic-group substratum effect.

A similar kind of substratum effect can be found in the English of Scotland. Most Scots today tend to think of themselves as simply 'Scottish', but historically speaking they represent descendants of two distinct ethnic groups. To simplify things somewhat, we can say that Highland Scots were Gaels, and spoke Gaelic (as many of them still do in the West Highlands and on the islands of the Hebrides), while Lowland Scots were English speakers. Now that English is spoken by nearly everyone in Scotland, this difference still survives in the type of English one can hear in different parts of the country. Lowland Scots speak either a local dialect or standard English with a local accent (or something in between). Highlanders, on the other hand, speak either standard Scots English (which the group as a whole initially learnt as a foreign language) or something not too far removed from this – not nearly so far from it as the Lowland dialects, in any case. (Highlanders do not normally say *I dinna ken*, for example, but rather *I don't know*.) There is often, however, a certain amount of substratum influence from Gaelic in the English spoken by Highlanders which may identify them as coming from the Highlands. Native speakers of Gaelic, of course, will often have a Gaelic accent in English, but one can detect lexical and grammatical differences even in the speech of Highlanders who have never spoken Gaelic in their lives. Examples include differences such as the following:

West Highland English	Standard Scots English
Take that whisky here.	*Bring that whisky here.*
I'm seeing you!	*I can see you!*
It's not that that I'm wanting.	*I don't want that.*

In the English-speaking world as a whole one of the most striking examples of linguistic ethnic-group differentiation – and one where the postulated role of some kind of substratum effect is a controversial subject – is the difference we have already noted between the speech of black and white Americans. These differences are by no means manifest in the speech of all Americans, but they are sufficiently widespread to be of considerable interest and importance. It was recognized a long time ago that black Americans spoke English differently from the whites. A British visitor writing in 1746 said of the American colonists, 'One thing they are very faulty in, with regard to their children . . . is that when young, they suffer them too much to prowl among the young Negroes, which insensibly causes them to imbibe their manners and broken speech.' Differences, then, were noted, and were generally held to be the result of inherent mental or physical differences between the two ethnic groups. Since the English which black people spoke was felt, as the above quotation shows, to be debased or corrupt, the difference was also considered to be the result – and indeed proof – of the inherent inferiority of black people (a fashionable belief at the time). Negroes, it was thought, could not 'speak English properly' since they were simply not capable of it. This view has no basis in fact, but it cannot be altogether ignored, even today: it was at one time so widely held that it has affected the history of the study of Negro American English. Many developments in this field have to be viewed against this historical background, and the subject as a whole is in any case fraught with various social and political implications.

The influence of this earlier view lingered on in the following way: since differences in black speech had formerly been ascribed to racial inferiority, the recognition that there was in fact *no* inferiority seemed to imply to linguists who might have thought of studying Negro English that black speech was not (and could not be) different. This meant that no one could study black speech as such without appearing to be racialist, and the subject was therefore neglected for many years. Eventually, however, linguists realized that this attitude was the ethnic-group counterpart to the view, recognized as false, that differences between *social* dialects implied linguistic superiority of one variety over another. If Negroes and whites spoke differently, this simply meant that there were different (linguistically equally good) ethnic-group language varieties. Today, therefore, linguists are agreed that there are differences between Negro speech and white speech and, since there is no way in which one variety can be linguistically superior to another, that it is not racialist to say so. The political and social climate is now such that this linguistic problem can be extensively studied and discussed. In fact, such a store of interesting data has been uncovered in the past few years that the study of 'black English' or 'non-standard Negro English (NNE)' or 'black English vernacular (BEV)' is now one of the major preoccupations of many American linguists. These three terms are generally used to refer to the non-standard English spoken by lower-class blacks in the urban ghettoes of the northern USA and elsewhere. *Black English*, as a linguistic term, has the disadvantage that it suggests that all blacks speak this one variety of English – which is not the case. *NNE* and *BEV*, on the other hand, distinguish those blacks who speak standard American English from those who do not, although they still suggest that only one variety, homogeneous throughout the whole of the USA, is involved, which is hardly likely, in spite of a surprising degree of similarity between geographically separated varieties. Some of the more typical grammatical characteristics of BEV are exemplified in the following passages:

TWELVE-YEAR-OLD BOY, DETROIT: 'Sometimes we think she's absolutely crazy. She come in the classroom she be nice and happy ... the next minute she be hollering at us for no reason, she never have a smile, she'd be giving us a lecture on something that happened twenty years ago.' (From the survey of Detroit speech led by Roger Shuy.)

FIFTEEN-YEAR-OLD HARLEM BOY: 'You know, like some people say if you're good your spirit goin' t'heaven ... 'n' if you bad, your spirit goin' to hell. Well, bullshit! Your spirit goin' to hell anyway. I'll tell you why. 'Cause, you see, doesn' nobody really know that it's a God. An' when they be sayin' if you good, you goin' t'heaven, tha's bullshit, 'cause you ain't goin' to no heaven, 'cause it ain't no heaven for you to go to.' (From a survey of New York speech led by William Labov.)

In any case, although BEV is now recognized in academic linguistic circles as a normal, valid and interesting variety (or varieties) of English, controversy still remains. While it is recognized that there are differences between BEV and other varieties, there is disagreement as to the nature of these differences and, in particular, to their origin. One view is that all features which are said to be characteristic of BEV can also be found in white speech, although not necessarily in the same combination, and particularly in the white speech of the southern states of the USA. Most features of BEV, this view claims, are therefore derived historically from British or other white dialects. They have come to be interpreted as 'black English' because black people have emigrated from the south to the northern cities of the USA, so that what were originally geographical differences have now become, in the north, ethnic-group differences. (There are parallels here, of course, with the Serbo-Croat of Sarajevo.) Furthermore, it is also possible that racial segregation and the growth of ghettoes, which have meant that there has been only minimal contact between blacks and whites, have led to the independent development of the English of the two groups – that the two varieties have generated their own distinct linguistic innovations.

The other view claims that many, at least, of the characteristics of BEV can be explained by supposing that the first American Negroes spoke some kind of English Creole. (I shall leave a full discussion of creole languages until Chapter 7, pp. 170–180. Simply put, however, the term *creole* is applied to a pidgin language which has become the native language of a speech community, and has therefore become expanded again, and acquired all the functions and characteristics of a full natural language. A pidgin is a reduced, simplified, often mixed language evolved for, say, trading purposes by speakers with no common language. Varieties of English Creole (that is, creolized Pidgin English) are widely spoken in the West Indies by people of African descent. In their 'purest' form they are not immediately comprehensible to English speakers, although the vocabulary is similar, and they show fairly considerable influence from African languages.) The hypothesis is, then, that BEV is not derived from British English dialects, but rather from an English Creole much like that of, say, Jamaica. This view would hold that the earliest American Negroes had a creole as their native language, and that this has, over the years, come to resemble more and more closely the language of the whites. In other words, while the language of American blacks should clearly now be referred to as *English*, those places where BEV differs from other English varieties are the result of continuing creole influence. Adherents of this view also suggest that similarities between the speech of blacks and southern whites may be due to the influence of the former on the latter, rather than vice versa. (There are some clear cases of lexical items which have been introduced into American English from African languages, e.g. *voodoo, pinto* 'coffin', *goober* 'peanut'.)

Let us attempt a short review of the evidence. We shall select some of the most frequently cited characteristics of BEV, beginning with certain phonological features, and then see how they can best be explained.

1. Many black speakers do not have postvocalic /r/ in *cart* or *car*. This feature can quite clearly be traced back to British dialects, and it is also, of course, a feature found in the speech of many American whites. Many lower-class Negroes, however, also demonstrate loss of intervocalic /r/ (that is, /r/ between vowels) in words like *Carol* and *Paris* (*Ca'ol, Pa'is*), so that *Paris* and *pass*, *parrot* and *pat* may be homophonous (i.e., sound the same). This feature, though not nearly so commonly, can be heard in the speech of certain southern whites (British readers will perhaps be familiar with this sort of pronunciation from Westerns: *Howdy she'iff!*), and there are also speakers of British RP who can be heard, for example, to say *very* and similar words with no /r/: *ve'y nice*. Some Negro speakers also show loss of /r/ after initial consonants, in certain cases, e.g. *f'om = from, p'otect = protect*. This last may be peculiar to BEV.

2. Many black speakers often do not have /θ/, as in *thing*, or /ð/, as in *that*. In initial position they may be merged with /t/ (rarely) and /d/ respectively, so that *this* is *dis*, for example. This feature is also found, to a certain extent, in the speech of white Americans, but not, it appears, nearly so frequently. It is worth noting that it is also a feature of Caribbean creoles. In other positions, /θ/ and /ð/ may be merged with /f/ and /v/, so that pronunciations such as *b'uvvuh* /bəvə/, for 'brother', may occur. This feature is well-known in London speech. It also occurs in other British varieties, and in the speech of whites in Kentucky.

3. All English speakers, in their normal speech, simplify final consonant clusters in words like *lost, west, desk, end* or *cold* (where both consonants are either voiceless or voiced), where another consonant follows: *los' time, wes' coast*. Where a vowel follows, however, simplification does not occur: *lost elephant,*

west end. In BEV, on the other hand, simplification can take place in all environments, so that pronunciations like *los' elephant*, *wes' en'* may occur. This means that, in BEV, plurals of nouns ending in standard English in *-st*, *-sp* and *-sk* are often formed on the pattern of *class: classes* rather than of *clasp: clasps*. For example, the plural of *desk* may be *desses*, the plural of *test*, *tesses*. Consonant-cluster reduction of this type is also a feature of Caribbean creoles, but it appears, too, to be common in the speech of whites in some parts of the South. However, there also seems to be at least one respect in which some types of BEV are unique. While some whites say *tes'* and others *test*, they all have forms like *tester* and *testing*: where the cluster is followed by a suffix beginning with a vowel, simplification does not take place. This is also usual with black speakers, particularly in the North, but there are some Negroes, particularly southern children, who have *tessing* and *tesser*. In other words, the form of items of this type must be assumed to be *tess* for these speakers since they never have a *t* in any context. We can say, then, that there are some BEV speakers who, like creole speakers, do not have final consonant clusters of the type *-st*.

4. A number of other features are characteristic of BEV pronunciation. They include the nasalization of vowels before nasal consonants and the subsequent loss of the consonant: *run, rum, rung* = [rə̃]; vocalization and loss of postvocalic /l/: *told* may be pronounced identically with *toe*; and devoicing of final /b/, /d/, /g/ (*bud* and *but* may be distinguished only by the slightly longer vowel of the former) and possible loss of final /d/: *toad* may be pronounced identically with *toe*. All these features, with the possible exception of the last, can be found in various white varieties of English.

Perhaps more central to this argument about the origin of differences between BEV and other forms of English are grammatical differences.

1. Many black speakers do not have *-s* in third-person singular present-tense forms, so that forms such as *he go*, *it come*, *she like* are usual. We saw in Chapter 2, however, that this is a feature of certain British dialects (it is widespread in East Anglia and in

parts of the West Country), and also occurs in the speech of many (particularly southern) white Americans. A certain amount of research, however, has nevertheless suggested that we cannot necessarily ascribe this BEV feature to an origin in white speech. It has been shown that, in Mississippi, there is a significant difference between the speech of black and white children from the lowest social-class groups with respect to this feature. All the white children studied used some -s in the appropriate verb forms, and the average score for the group as a whole was 85 per cent -s usage. On the other hand, only 76 per cent of the black children used any -s, and the overall average score for -s usage was only 13 per cent. There are two possible interpretations of these figures. One interpretation is that both varieties are inherently variable with respect to -s, and that – as we have seen to be the case with class dialects – it is simply the proportions of -s usage that are different. A second interpretation is that, leaving aside the variety spoken by the white children, the black children speak a variety of English which, like English Creoles, has no -s. The few cases where black children do use the standard English form (13 per cent), this interpretation would hold, are the result of dialect mixture – the influence of standard English. Even this second interpretation, however, does not necessarily indicate a creole origin for BEV – we saw in Chapter 2 that LWC Norwich speakers too are almost invariable in the use of forms without -s.

2. An important grammatical characteristic of BEV is the absence of the copula – the verb *to be* – in the present tense. This characteristic is central to the present controversy. In BEV, as in Russian, Hungarian, Thai and many other languages including, crucially, creoles, the following type of sentence is grammatical:

> *She real nice.*
> *They out there.*
> *He not American.*
> *If you good, you going to heaven.*

(Where the copula appears in 'exposed' position, as in *I know what it is*, or *Is she?*, it is always present.) What is the origin of this feature in BEV? Dialectologists point out that in some varieties of white English copula absence is grammatical. Creolists, on the other hand, point out that the English Creoles of the Caribbean have invariable copula absence. The creolists' case appears to be strong. The same Mississippi study we discussed above, for example, shows that copula deletion in white southern speech, although it does occur, is hardly of the same order as this phenomenon in black speech. While black children deleted *is* in nearly 28 per cent of cases, white children lacked *is* less than 2 per cent of the time. Similarly, blacks deleted *are* in 77 per cent of cases, while whites showed deletion in only 21 per cent of cases. Advocates of the creole origin of copula deletion in BEV can therefore point to the fact (a) that copula deletion does not occur in British dialects, (b) that copula absence is a feature of English-based creoles spoken by Negroes in the Caribbean and (c) that it is much more common in the speech of American blacks than American whites. (They might also like to suggest that copula deletion in white American – but not British – English is the result of influence from BEV.) Opponents of this view, on the other hand, can point to another crucial problem: is copula deletion in BEV a grammatical or a phonological phenomenon? Is the copula, that is, 'not there' in BEV, or is it 'there' but not pronounced? BEV, as we have seen, is frequently characterized by absence of postvocalic /r/. Is, therefore, the deletion of *are* simply an example of this same phenomenon – is *they're* > *they* an example of the same phenomenon as *car* > *cah*? A further point to bear in mind is that, as other linguists have pointed out, BEV deletes the copula only in those contexts where standard English contracts it – where *is* becomes *'s* or *are* becomes *'re*. It is therefore possible to conclude that copula deletion may be a phonological innovation of BEV which continues the older process of deletion, thus: *he is* > *he's* > *he; they are* > *they're* > *they*.

3. Perhaps the most important characteristic of BEV is the so-called 'invariant *be*': the use of the form *be* as a finite verb form. For example,

He usually be around.
Sometime she be fighting.
Sometime when they do it, most of the problems always
be wrong.
She be nice and happy.
They sometimes be incomplete.

At first sight, this use of *be* appears to be no different from its occurrence in certain British dialects, where *I be, he be* etc. correspond to standard English *I am, he is*. There is, however, a crucial difference between BEV and all other varieties of English. As the adverbs *usually* and *sometimes* in the above sentences show, invariant *be* is used in BEV only to indicate 'habitual aspect' – it is only used to refer to some event that is repeated and is not continuous. There is therefore a verbal contrast in BEV which is not possible in standard English.

BEV	Standard English
He busy right now.	*He's busy right now.*
Sometime he be busy.	*Sometimes he's busy.*

In standard English the verb form is the same in both cases, whereas they are distinct in BEV because, while the first sentence does not refer to some repeated non-continuous action, the second does. In BEV, constructions such as *He be busy right now* and *He be my father* are not grammatical sentences. (The latter would imply, 'He is only my father from time to time.') This kind of distinction in the verb is certainly reminiscent of creole languages. In Caribbean creoles, verb aspect – the distribution of an event through time (whether it is repeated, continuous, completed, and so on) – tends to be of greater importance than tense – the actual location of an event in time (see p. 177). At the same time, it should be said that this sort of habitual–non-habitual distinction is not unknown in British dialects, although where it does occur it does so in by no means exactly the same form. In the old-fashioned dialect of Dorset, for example, *He beat her*, meaning 'He beat her on one particular occasion in the past,' contrasts with *He did beat her*, meaning that he was in the habit of doing so. There are, however, two other respects in which the aspectual system of BEV differs from that of standard English (and more closely resembles that of some creoles). BEV and standard English have in common a present perfect verb form, *I have talked*, and past perfect form, *I had talked*. But BEV has, in addition, two further forms: *I done talked*, which has been called 'completive aspect', indicating that the action is completed; and *I been talked*, the 'remote aspect', indicating an event that occurred in the remote past. Completive aspect can be found in certain white dialects, but the remote aspect appears to be peculiar to BEV (although it is not, it must be said, particularly common even there).

4. Three final grammatical characteristics of BEV worthy of mention are: BEV question inversion, 'existential *it*', and 'negativized auxiliary pre-position'. Rules for question inversion in indirect questions in BEV differ from those in standard English, and result in sentences such as *I asked Mary where did she go* and *I want to know did he come last night*. Existential *it* occurs where standard English has *there*. For example, *It's a boy in my class name Joey*; *It ain't no heaven for you to go to*; *Doesn't nobody know that it's a God*. This last sentence also illustrates negativized auxiliary pre-position. In BEV, if a sentence has a negative indefinite like *nobody, nothing*, then the negative auxiliary (*doesn't, can't*) can be placed at the beginning of the sentence: *Can't nobody do nothing about it; Wasn't nothing wrong with that* (with statement intonation).

To summarize, there are four possible views one can take with respect to the controversy about the origins of BEV, depending on which of the two views one accepts on its origins, and what one considers the present-day situation to be.

1. The 'different-equals-inferior' view maintains that there are no differences between the speech of black and white Americans and that, therefore, all characteristics of BEV can be traced back to British dialects or are American innovations that also occur in white speech in the USA. Most linguists would not now accept this view, since it has been demonstrated to their satisfaction that there are some significant differences. The view still

has its adherents outside linguistics, however. Because of the legacy of the 'different-equals-inferior' position, some black people still feel that the academic discussion of BEV is an attempt to discriminate against them, and would prefer that the subject not be discussed. This is not altogether surprising in view of the prejudices many people still have about language, and it is noteworthy that even militant black leaders, while content to use 'black slang' as an in-group language, have made no reference to BEV as, say, a dialect to be proud of. As recently as 1949, one writer claimed that Negroes 'could not pronounce r' because of their 'thick lips'. (He was presumably referring to the lack in BEV, as in RP, of postvocalic /r/. How Negroes are able to articulate prevocalic /r/ he does not explain.) This view is clearly absurd, but it still colours people's attitudes to this subject.

2. The 'dialectologist' view recognizes that there are differences between BEV and white speech but claims, nevertheless, that BEV is historically derived from British dialects. This view is popular with some American dialectologists, who suggest that the differences are due to a different *combination* of British dialect features; to the fact that BEV may have preserved certain archaic features now lost in other varieties; and to later, independent developments in the different varieties. They point out that it would be surprising, in view of the cultural division in America between whites and blacks, if their speech had not developed differently. They suggest, in particular, that the development of the urban ghetto and of barriers to communication imposed by poverty and deprivation have been instrumental in their development. Characteristics of white and black speech were originally the same, but have been 'skewed' by the colour–caste system. (This is one way of explaining the different proportions of -s usage in verbs in the two ethnic groups.) Against this view it has been pointed out that many of the characteristics said to be typical of ghetto speech can also be found in southern rural Negro speech. Opponents have also pointed out that there are dangers in the 'skewing' view: in particular, that it could be interpreted, by persons so inclined, as being due not only to economic deprivation, but also to some kind of biological inferiority.

3. The 'integrationist' view claims that, although historical records provide a certain amount of evidence to suggest that Negroes in America used to speak an African-influenced creole type of English, there are no longer any features of BEV which cannot be found in white speech. In other words, although there was formerly a difference, BEV and some types of southern white speech are now indistinguishable. This, it could be claimed, is due to the gradual convergence of creole English with English, and also to some influence of BEV on white speech. This view does not appear to have much support amongst linguists, but it will be obvious that the stressing of present-day similarities between black and white speech may find support from those who favour an 'integrationist' approach to America's racial problems.

4. The 'creolist' view maintains that there are (as most linguists are now agreed) significant differences between BEV and other varieties, and that these can be best explained in terms of the creole origins of BEV. BEV, that is, is an English Creole like those spoken in the Caribbean which has gradually become more and more decreolized. One piece of evidence that may support this view has been based on a particular feature of BEV syntax. In standard English and white varieties of non-standard English the following sentence types can occur:

Standard English: *We were eating – and drinking too.*
White non-standard: *We was eatin' – and drinkin' too.*

In these varieties it would be possible for a fuller form to occur: *We were eating – and we were drinking too*, but it is more normal to omit the pronoun *we* and the auxiliary *were* in the second clause. In many English Creoles, on the other hand, it is more usual to omit only the auxiliary. Consider the following translations of the above example into Gullah, an English Creole spoken in an isolated part of the coastal American South, Jamaican Creole, and Sranan, an English Creole spoken in Surinam:

Gullah: *We bin duh nyam – en' we duh drink, too.*
Jamaican C: *We ben a nyam – an' we a drink, too.*
Sranan: *We ben de nyang – en' we de dringie, too.*

(In this example *nyam* and *nyang* = *eat*, *bin* is the past tense marker or auxiliary – note the parallel with BEV *I been talked* – and *duh*, *a* and *de* are continuous aspect markers corresponding to English *-ing* forms.) Strikingly enough, the BEV form, although superficially more like the standard English and non-standard white English forms, is in fact basically more like the Creole examples in that it usually omits only the auxiliary:

BEV: *We was eatin' – an' we drinkin', too.*

My own view is that, even if many of the features of BEV can be found in various white dialects, BEV itself functions today as a separate ethnic-group variety which identifies its speakers as being black rather than white. Many of the features of BEV must be ascribed to the fact that the first Negroes in the United States spoke some kind of English Creole – the resemblances between BEV and West Indian creoles are at some points too striking to ignore. This, however, does not necessarily indicate that other features of BEV may not be traceable directly to British dialects. In some cases, for instance, archaisms lost in white speech may be preserved in BEV. In other cases, the controversy about the origins of BEV may be rather meaningless. Verb forms like *he love*, *she do* can probably be explained as the result of creole background *and* British dialect influence, the one reinforcing the other. And it is worth remembering, too, that English Creoles themselves are historically also derived partly from British dialects.

The differences between BEV and standard English, whatever their origin, are quite large, and in some respects fairly fundamental. Now, we hypothesized at the end of Chapter 2 that the fact that the language of schools was standard English could make for certain difficulties for children who were native speakers of a non-standard variety. We suggested that this was likely to be at least a partial explanation for the relative educational failure of many working-class children – not because of any inherent deficiency in their language but only because their language is different from the standard. In view of the marked differences between BEV and standard English, therefore, it is not surprising that a considerable amount of attention has now been focused in the USA on the educational implications of the language used by Negro children. A number of linguists have been carrying out a considerable amount of work in this field that has importance for linguists, educationalists and teachers, not only in the USA, but also for those in other parts of the English-speaking world where there are large differences between non-standard varieties and standard English (for example, the West Indies and the Lowlands of Scotland).

One obvious problem is that speakers of BEV, like other non-standard speakers, are presented with greater difficulties in learning to read and, in particular, to write than are children who are standard English speakers: not only do they have to learn the mechanics of reading and writing, they also have to learn standard English, since this is the variety of English that is normally used in writing. In some cases the difficulties the child experiences are the result of purely phonological (accent) differences. Many BEV speakers, for example, do not distinguish *pin* and *pen*, *tin* and *ten* that is, the contrast between /ɪ/ and /e/ is neutralized before /n/. This means that children with accents of this type may have some problems in learning to write *pin* and *pen* correctly. There is nothing unusual in this problem, however. All English speakers have to learn to write differently words which they pronounce the same. (Most English speakers pronounce *beat* and *beet*, *meat* and *meet* the same, for example.) The only possible difficulty here, therefore, is if the teacher is not aware of the problem. All teachers know about the *meat–meet* problem. But it is quite likely that many white middle-class American teachers will not be aware of the BEV speakers *pen–pin* problem. They may therefore (a) interpret a reading of *pin* which to them sounds like *pen* as a reading mistake, which it is not, and (b) be unaware of the difficulties involved in getting children to spell words of this type correctly. The general principle to follow here is, therefore, that teachers should be as familiar as possible with the phonological structure of their children's language. (In some cases accent difficulties will be much greater than this. The Lowland Scottish child who natively says /heːm/ *hame* for 'home' will have to learn that there is another pronunciation of this word, /hoːm/, before he can learn to interpret the symbols of *home* correctly.)

In other cases it may not be so clear whether the problem is a grammatical or phonological one. For example, if a child speaker of BEV says

> *I pass by the school yesterday,*

this could indicate one of three different things:

 (i) the child has no concept of past tense;
 (ii) he has a concept of past tense, but the *-ed* suffix does not function for him as a marker of this tense;
(iii) the *-ed* functions and is understood as a marker of past tense, but does not actually appear in speech because of final consonant cluster simplification (i.e. it is a phonological phenomenon see p. 68).

The first possibility can be ruled out straight away, it seems, since all BEV speakers normally alternate forms like *go* with *went*, *know* with *knew* and *keep* with *kept*. It is not immediately clear, however, whether black children who are native speakers of BEV actually have an *-ed* suffix (which is not pronounced) or whether they do not have one at all – are we dealing with (ii) or (iii)? Clearly, the answer to this question will be of considerable importance to teaching strategy, and to an understanding of a child's reading and writing problems. In order to investigate this problem further several tests have been carried out with children from ghetto schools. One of the most interesting of these tests was based on the fortunate fact that the orthographic form *read* is a homograph in English: it can be pronounced /riːd/ (present tense) or /rɛd/ (past tense). A reading test was devised as follows. Some BEV-speaking children were, first, asked to read sentences like:

> *Last month I read five books.*
> *Now I read and write better than Alfred.*

This established whether they could use time indicators like *last month* and *now* to produce the correct reading of read – /rɛd/

and /riːd/ respectively. They were then asked to read out sentences such as:

> *When I passed by, I read the posters.*
> *When I liked a story, I read every word.*
> *I looked for trouble when I read the news.*

In the first half of these sentences the child meets the *-ed* suffix. If he interprets the suffix as an indication of past tense (whether or not he actually pronounces it, which is a rather different matter), *read* will be pronounced /rɛd/. If not, then it is quite likely that he will read it as /riːd/. The results of the test showed that, while there were some children who interpreted *-ed* correctly, a majority did not: for many black ghetto children, *-ed* does not function as a marker of the past tense. It is therefore useful for the teacher of BEV-speaking children to decide which of the two categories her children come into. Suppose a child reads out *he passed by* as [hi pæs baɪ]. This can indicate one of two things. The apparent reading mistake may simply be, instead, a pronunciation difference: the child may have a different set of homonyms from the teacher in that he pronounces *passed* and *pass* the same. For him, *pass* and *passed* are different words with different meanings which, like *meat* and *meet*, are not actually distinguished in pronunciation. The child has performed the reading task correctly, and has understood the sentence. In this case there is no point in the teacher correcting [pæs] to [pæst]. (A parallel case would be if a teacher from the south of England accused a northern child of misreading *cud* as *could* when he had in fact produced a correct reading of *cud*.) On the other hand, it might mean that the child has no recognition of *-ed* as a past-tense marker, and that the *-ed* is for him simply a group of meaningless 'silent letters'. It is obviously essential for the teacher to distinguish clearly between the two cases. In the second case she will have to get the child to interpret orthographic *-ed* as a past-tense marker. (She need *not* teach him what past tense is *nor* teach him to say [pæst] rather than [pæs] – his actual pronunciation is immaterial.) In any case, it is important that the teacher should have a knowledge of the child's native variety so that, with an appreciation of what are the homonyms of this variety, she can judge what are and are not reading mistakes. (It is also, incidentally, important that those engaged in preparing reading materials should be aware of these problems: they should allow for the fact that the Scots child will not distinguish words from the sets of *cot* and *caught* or *pool* and *pull*; that the East Anglian child may not distinguish *who* and *Hugh*, or *boot* and *boat*; or the Yorkshire child *put* and *putt*. They should also allow for the fact that many English speakers *do* distinguish pairs like *their* and *there*, *berth* and *birth*, *nose* and *knows*, *days* and *daze*, *beet* and *beat*.)

Reading, however, is only one aspect of this language problem. If children are going to read, then they have to learn, for the moment at least, to read standard English. There is no question about this. But what of the language the children actually use themselves? If BEV-speaking children and other non-standard-English-speaking children suffer educationally because standard English is not their native language, then what steps can be taken to solve this problem? So far it is possible to distinguish three different approaches that have been adopted to this problem. The first approach has been described as 'elimination of non-standard speech'. In this approach, traditional in most parts of the English-speaking world and still quite widespread, every attempt is made in the schools to prevent the child from speaking his native non-standard variety, and each non-standard feature of which the teacher is aware is commented on and corrected. For example, the child will be told that it is 'wrong' (and perhaps even bad or a disgrace) to say *I done it, I ain't got it*, or *He a good guy*. Standard English, on the other hand, is presented as 'correct' and 'good' – the model to be aimed at. Pupils who attain proficiency in standard English are often considered more favourably than those who do not.

Linguists, and many others, believe this approach to be wrong, for several reasons. First, it is wrong *psychologically*. Language, as we have seen, is not simply a means of communicating messages. It is also very important as a symbol of identity and group membership. To suggest to a child that his language, and that of those with whom he identifies, is inferior in some way is to imply that *he* is inferior. This, in turn, is likely to lead either to alienation from the school and school values, or to a rejection of the group to which he belongs. It is also *socially* wrong in that it may appear to imply that particular social groups are less valuable than others. This is particularly undesirable when the language being stigmatized is that of lower-class black children and the one which is being extolled is that of white middle-class adult teachers. Finally, and perhaps most importantly, it is *practically* wrong: it is wrong because it does not and will not work. To learn a new language is a very difficult task, as many people know, and in many ways it is even more difficult to learn a different dialect of one's own language – because they are so similar, it is difficult to keep them apart. The fact must also be faced that, in very many cases, speakers will not *want* to change their language – even if it were possible. First, there are no communication advantages to be gained (as there would be in learning French, for example) since the child was already able to communicate with standard English speakers anyway. Second, the pressures of group identification and peer-group solidarity are very strong. Linguistic research has shown that the adolescent peer-group is in many cases the most important linguistic influence. Children do not grow up speaking like their parents, and they certainly do not grow up speaking like their teachers – their speech patterns are those of their friends. In other words, time spent in the classroom trying to eradicate non-standard speech is wasted time. If children suffer because they speak non-standard English, the solution is not to eliminate the non-standard varieties.

The second approach has been called 'bidialectalism', and has received the overt support of many linguists. This approach teaches that the individual has a right to continue using a non-standard dialect at home, with friends, and in certain circumstances at school. But it also advocates that children should be taught standard English as a school language, and as the language of reading and writing. The two varieties, standard and non-standard, are discussed and treated as distinct entities, and the differences between them are illustrated and pointed out as an interesting fact. The aims are to encourage the child's interest in language by study of his own dialect as a legitimate and interesting form of language, and to help the child to develop an ability in *code-switching* – switching from one language variety to another when the situation demands (something most non-standard-English-speaking children are often quite good at anyway). This approach recognizes the appropriateness of BEV and other non-standard varieties for peer-group interaction and other functions, and respects the child's feelings about his own language. For best results it requires that the teacher have some knowledge of the linguistic correlates of social stratification, and of the child's dialect. It also concentrates solely on grammatical and vocabulary features. (Of course, it may be valuable to point out to children that some accents are more highly valued than others – but also that this is a social, not a linguistic fact.) It seems that this approach is likely to be successful, for the most part, only with writing, which is a more conscious and less automatic activity than speaking. In general, what the teacher does in the classroom with respect to spoken standard English will probably be irrelevant – because of the social and psychological factors we have outlined above. Children will learn to speak standard English, which is a dialect associated with and symbolic of a particular social group in our society, only if they both want to become a member of that group *and* have a reasonable expectation that it will be possible, economically and socially, for them to do so.

The third approach, which appears to be obtaining growing (but still minority) support in America, has been called 'appreciation of dialect differences'. This view states that if children suffer because of their non-standard language, this is due to the attitudes society as a whole, and perhaps teachers in particular, have to language of this type. If this is the case, then it is the attitudes that should be changed, and not the language. In other words, the problem is not really a linguistic one at all. We should, according to this approach, teach children the ability to read standard English, but, beyond that, we should simply attempt to educate our society to an understanding, appreciation and tolerance of non-standard dialects as complex, valid and adequate linguistic systems. Critics of this approach have called it hopelessly utopian. Given time, however, it might prove to be simpler than the other two approaches, since it may be easier to change attitudes than to alter the native speech patterns of the majority of the population. Education towards tolerance could be carried out in schools – but only by teachers free from language prejudice (who may in the end find it more rewarding – and perhaps morally more defensible – than teaching standard English). Supporters of this approach would hope, in the long run, for a situation where native speakers would no longer believe that they 'can't speak English'. But what of the short run? As other critics have pointed out, in the short run we may not be able to afford to abandon the bidialectalism approach. Until the degree of tolerance at which the third approach aims has been achieved, BEV speakers and other children with no ability in standard English will continue to be at a disadvantage. For this reason, to advocate the employment of the third approach alone may be to neglect the needs of these children. From the point of view of the linguist, therefore, the most satisfactory solution to the problem of non-standard speakers in a standard-English-dominated culture is the adoption in schools of a combination of the two approaches, bidialectalism and appreciation of dialect differences, bearing in mind that bidialectalism is likely to be only partially successful (and then probably only in the case of writing) and may be dangerous, particularly if insensitively handled, from the point of view of fostering linguistic insecurity.

4. Language and Sex

So far in this book we have been discussing some of the relationships to be found in linguistic communities between social differentiation and linguistic differentiation, together with some of the forms this linguistic differentiation can take. The two main types of social differentiation we have dealt with so far have been social stratification and ethnic-group differentiation. In both these cases we were able to point to parallels between social differentiation and geographical differentiation with respect to their effects on language: social distance, it appears, has the same kind of linguistic consequences as geographical distance. Ethnic and social-class groups, like regional groups, have linguistic characteristics in common because their members communicate more frequently with each other than with outsiders.

In this chapter, we shall be dealing with an aspect of linguistic differentiation that does not appear to be susceptible to the same kind of explanation. It is known from linguistic research that in many societies the speech of men and women differs. In some cases the differences are quite small and are not generally noticed: they are probably taken for granted in the same way as, say, different gestures or facial expressions. For example, in many accents of American English it has been found that women's vowels are more peripheral (more front, more back, higher, or lower) than men's. In other cases the differences may be quite large, overtly noted, and perhaps even actively taught to young children. In Gros Ventre, for example, an American Indian language from the north-eastern USA, palatalized dental stops in men's speech correspond to palatalized velar stops in the speech of women – men: /djatsa/; women: /kjatsa/ 'bread'. Again, in Yukaghir, a north-east Asian language, /tj/ and /dj/ in male speech correspond to /ts/ and /dz/ in the speech of women. We can be fairly sure in this last case that these differences are consciously made, since they also correlate with *age* differences: children also use the female /ts/ and /dz/ forms, while old people of both sexes use yet another set of variants, /čj/, /jj/. This means that a male speaker uses three different forms in the course of his lifetime, and is presumably therefore aware of the two change-overs that he makes.

Generally speaking, we cannot explain differences of this kind in terms of social distance. In most societies men and women communicate freely with one another, and there appear to be few social barriers likely to influence the density of communication between the sexes. We cannot, therefore, account for the development of sex varieties in language in the same way as class, ethnic-group, or geographical dialects. How, then, *do* such differences arise? Why do men and women often speak differently? Let us take a few examples of the kind of differences that have been reported, and attempt to see what factors may have been important in their development. We begin with some of the larger, overtly recognized differences.

The classic example of linguistic sex differentiation, well-known to students of language, comes from the West Indies. It was often reported that when Europeans first arrived in the Lesser Antilles and made contact with the Carib Indians who lived there, they discovered that the men and women 'spoke different languages'. This would of course have been a very startling discovery, and one that does not appear to have been paralleled anywhere else in the world: nowhere else has sex differentiation been found to be so great that people have been led to propose that there were actually distinct men and women's languages. However, it does seem that these reports (or later embellishments of them) were stretching things somewhat. A contemporary report (from the seventeenth century) says:

The men have a great many expressions peculiar to them, which the women understand but never pronounce themselves. On the other hand the women have words and phrases which the men never use, or they would be laughed to scorn. Thus it happens that in their conversations it often seems as if the women had another language than the men.

From the evidence supplied by this seventeenth-century writer, as well as from the above quotation, it seems certain that, although there were clear differences between men and women's speech, only a relatively small number of vocabulary items were involved. The men and women, that is, did *not* speak different languages. Rather, they spoke different varieties of the same language – the differences were lexical only. Even so, how can we explain these particular differences? The Indians themselves had an explanation which has also been quite widely accepted. The contemporary report quoted above continues:

The savage natives of Dominica say that the reason for this is that when the Caribs came to occupy the islands these were inhabited by an Arawak tribe which they exterminated completely, with the exception of the women, whom they married in order to populate the country. It is asserted that there is some similarity between the speech of the continental Arawaks and that of the Carib women.

The differences, that is, were believed to be the result of the mixing of two language groups, Carib and Arawak, divided on sex lines, as the result of an invasion. This may or may not be true, and it is probably unlikely that we shall ever know what the origin of these differences was. One thing is clear, however: even if this explanation is true, we cannot apply it to the origin of sex dialects in other parts of the world. We must also regard the 'invasion' theory, even in this particular case, as rather suspect. First, the reported differences amongst the Carib Indians resemble to a considerable extent those found elsewhere in other American Indian languages. Secondly, the linguist Otto Jespersen has advanced another explanation which is, at least, equally plausible and which will perhaps apply (as we would wish) to other cases as well. Jespersen suggests that sex differentiation, in some cases, may be the result of the phenomenon of *taboo* which we discussed in Chapter 1. He points out that it is known that when Carib men were on the war-path they would use a number of words which only adult males were allowed to employ. If women or uninitiated boys used these words, bad luck was considered likely to result. Taboo may perhaps therefore have a powerful influence on the growth of separate sex vocabularies generally. If taboos become associated with particular objects or activities such that, say, women are not permitted to use the original name, then new words or paraphrases are likely to be used instead, and sex differentiation of vocabulary items will result. Examples of taboo as an explanatory factor come also from other parts of the world. In Zulu, for example, it has been reported that a wife was not allowed to mention the name of her father-in-law or his brothers, and she might be put to death if she broke this taboo. Moreover, we saw in Chapter 1 that taboo can extend to words which simply resemble the original tabooed words. In Zulu, it appears that this process could go so far as to include particular sounds of the language. Say, for example, that the tabooed name contained the sound /z/. This might mean, apparently, that the woman in question would not be able to use a word like *amanzi* 'water' without converting it to a form without the tabooed sound, *amandabi*. If this kind of process became generalized to all the women in the community, then it can be seen that distinct sex dialects might result.

Taboo, however, is not a particularly good explanation of sex dialects. First, it is not really clear how differences of the above type could become generalized to the whole community. And secondly, in many other cases it is quite clear that we are not dealing with taboo. In some of these cases the explanation is quite readily apparent. For example, in Chiquito, an American Indian language of Bolivia, if a woman wants to say 'my brother' she says *ičibausi*, whereas a male speaker would say *tsaruki*. This, however, does not constitute a sex-dialect difference of the same order as those we have already discussed; rather it is a result of the Chiquito kinship and gender systems. Just as we distinguish in English between the sex of close relations referred to or addressed (*brother*, *sister*, *uncle*, *aunt*), so many other languages also have different terms according to the sex of the speaker doing the referring or addressing. This is simply a recognition of the fact that the relationship brother–sister is different from the relationship brother–brother. Other relationships in Chiquito are differentiated in the same way:

	male speaker	female speaker
my father	*ijai*	*išupu*
my mother	*ipaki*	*ipapa*

This sort of differentiation is similar to that found in the pronominal systems. In English we differentiate between the sexes only in the third-person singular: *he, she.* In French the third-person plural is also differentiated: *ils, elles,* while in Finnish there is no distinction even in the singular: *hän* can be equivalent to either *he* or *she.* In other languages of the world, sex differentiation extends to the second person and even to the first person. In Thai, for example, in polite conversation between equals, a man will say *phom* for the first-person singular pronoun 'I' whereas a woman will refer to herself as *dichan.*

There are other cases where taboo is clearly not a factor, but where the explanation is not so simple as these gender and kinship examples. In research done in the 1930s, for example, quite notable sex differences were found in the American Indian language Koasati, a language of the Muskogean family, spoken in Louisiana. The differences, which seemed to be disappearing at the time the research was carried out, involved the phonological shapes of particular verb forms. Consider the following examples:

	male	female
'He is saying'	/kaːs/	/kãː/
'Don't lift it!'	/lakaučiːs/	/lakaučin/
'He is peeling it'	/mols/	/mol/
'You are building a fire'	/oːsč/	/oːst/

From this list the differences appear to be rather haphazard, but they are in fact entirely predictable according to a series of fairly complicated rules. (For example, if the female form ends in a nasalized vowel, then the male form has a non-nasalized vowel plus /s/, e.g. female /lakauwãː/; male /lakauwaːs/ 'He will lift it.') There is also good reason to believe that the same kind of differentiation formerly existed in other Muskogean languages, but that in these languages the women's varieties have died out. (This is partly confirmed by the fact that in Koasati itself it was only the older women who preserved the distinct forms. Younger women and girls used the male forms.) Differences of this kind have been found in a number of other American languages. In addition to the Gros Ventre case mentioned above, sex differences of some kind have been found in the American Indian languages Yana and Sioux, and in the Eskimo spoken in Baffin Island.

Taboo does not appear to be involved in any of these cases. The two varieties of Koasati, for example, were learnt from parents who were equally familiar with both and would correct children when necessary. If a small boy said /kã:/, for example, his mother would stop him and, herself using the male form, say, 'No, you must say /ka:s/.' No taboo prohibition prevented her from using this form. Similarly, when relating stories a man could quite properly use female forms when quoting a female character – and vice versa. Another example which helps to make this point comes from Darkhat Mongolian. The back rounded vowels /u/ and /o/ in men's speech correspond to the mid vowels /ʉ/ and /ʉ/ in women's speech, whereas male /ʉ/ and /ʉ/ correspond to female /y/ and /ø/ – front vowels. Although female speakers do not use /ʉ/ and /ʉ/ where male speakers use them, there is no taboo prohibition to prevent them from using these sounds in other cases:

Figure 3. Sex differentiation in Darkhat Mongolian

How *can* we explain differences of this type? In Koasati some, at least, of the female forms appeared to be *older* historically than the male forms. In other words, it seemed that linguistic changes had taken place in the male variety which had not been followed through (or were only just beginning to be followed) in the women's speech. The same sort of phenomenon occurs in other languages. Chukchi, for example, is a language spoken in Siberia. In some dialects, the female variety has intervocalic consonants in some words, particularly /n/ and /t/, which are not present in male forms; for example, male: /nitvaqaat/; female: /nitvaqenat/. Loss of intervocalic consonants is a much more frequent and expected sound change than the unmotivated insertion of consonants, and very many examples of loss of consonants in this position have been attested in languages from all parts of the world. This kind of distinction would therefore appear to provide a clear indication that the female variety is older than the male dialect. In more than one language, therefore, women's speech is more conservative than that of men.

Another clue comes, again, from Koasati, and in particular from the attitudes which the Koasati people themselves had to the two varieties. Older speakers, particularly the men, tended to say, when asked, that they thought the women's variety was *better* than that used by men. This is important, because it ties in in an interesting way with data we have from technologically more advanced speech communities. It also shows us that the sex varieties are not simply different: in at least two languages the male varieties are *innovating* and the female *conservative*, and in one case the female variety is evaluated as *better* as opposed to *worse*. Differences of this type should be easier to explain than linguistic differences, pure and simple.

Let us now take this discussion a stage further by examining some sex differences in English, where the differences are generally of the smaller, less obvious and more subconscious type. There are, it is true, a number of words and phrases which tend to be sex-bound. (Most of these, incidentally, seem to be exclamations of some sort. This suggests that taboo may be involved in some way: it is certainly more acceptable in our society for men to swear and use taboo words than it is for women.) Mostly, however, differences within English are phonetic and phonological, and taboo *cannot* be used as an explanation. The differences, moreover, are generally so insignificant that most people are not at all consciously aware of them. (Amongst RP speakers, for example, there is a greater tendency for women to have a glottal stop [ʔ] in consonant clusters of the type found in *simply* [sɪmʔplɪ] than for men.) Grammatical differences may also be involved, as we shall see below. Most of the evidence we have for sex varieties in English has come from some of the urban dialect surveys carried out in Britain and America that we have already mentioned. The sets of data these surveys have provided have one striking feature in common. In all the cases so far examined, it has been shown that, allowing for other factors such as social class, ethnic group and age, women consistently use forms which more closely approach those of the standard variety or the prestige accent than those used by men. In other words, female speakers of English, like their Koasati counterparts, use linguistic forms which are considered to be 'better' than male forms. In Chapter 2 we examined some of the ways in which linguistic variables are correlated with social class. These variables can also be used in the same sort of way to illustrate sex differentiation.

Consider the following figures. In Detroit, higher-class speakers use fewer instances of non-standard multiple negation (e.g. *I don't want none*) than lower-class speakers. Allowing for social class, however, women use fewer such forms than men do:

Percentage of multiple negation used

	UMC	LMC	UWC	LWC
Male	6.3	32.4	40.0	90.1
Female	0.0	1.4	35.6	58.9

In the case of the LMC and the LWC these differences are very big indeed: men are much more likely to say *I don't want none* than women are. Women, this suggests, are far more sensitive to the stigmatized nature of this grammatical feature than men. This sensitivity, moreover, is not confined to grammatical features. In the speech of Detroit Negroes, for instance, women use a far higher percentage of postvocalic /r/ (a prestige feature here as in New York) than men, allowing for social class:

Percentage of postvocalic /r/ in Detroit Negro speech

	UMC	LMC	UWC	LWC
Male	66.7	52.5	20.0	25.0
Female	90.0	70.0	44.2	31.7

Some writers have attempted to explain this sort of pattern in the black community by pointing out that the lower-class black ghetto family is typically matriarchal and that it is the mother of a family who conducts business with the outside world and who has job contacts with speakers of prestige varieties. This explanation is not adequate, however, since exactly the same pattern is found in the white community (where it tends to be the father who is in charge of external affairs) and in British English. In Norwich English, for example, the same sort of pattern emerges with the (ng) variable (whether speakers say *walking* or *walkin'*). The table below gives the percentage of non-RP-*in'* forms used by speakers in different class and sex groups:

	MMC	LMC	UWC	MWC	LWC
Male	4	27	81	91	100
Female	0	3	68	81	97

Once again, women use a higher percentage of 'better' forms than men do. In London English, too, men are more likely than women to use glottal stops in words like *butter* and *but*. And this phenomenon is not confined only to British and American English. In South Africa, for example, research has been carried out in the Transvaal, comparing the speech of male and female high-school pupils of the same age in the same town. A study was made of the pronunciation of four vowels:

1. The vowel of *gate,* which in South Africa ranges from high-prestige RP [geɪt] to low-prestige South African [gɜɪt], with a lower and more central first element to the diphthong, as in RP *bird*.
2. The vowel of *can't* which ranges from RP [kɑːnt] to South African [kɒːnt], with a vowel close in quality to that found in RP *on* – a low back rounded vowel.

3. The vowel of *out*, which ranges from RP [aut] to South African [æut], with a higher front first element resembling the vowel in RP *cat*.

4. The vowel in *boy*, which ranges from RP [bɔɪ] to a variant with a high back rounded first element [buɪ] as in RP *school*.

The results, giving the percentage of boys and girls using each variant in each case, are given below:

	RP	Non-RP		
gate	[geɪt]	[gɜɪt]		
boys	0	100		
girls	62	38		
can't	[kɑːnt]	[kɒːnt]		
boys	0	100		
girls	62	38		
out	[ɑut]	[aut]	[æut]	
boys	25	17	58	
girls	85	15	0	
boy	[bɔɪ]	[bɔɪ]	[boɪ]	[buɪ]
boys	0	16	42	42
girls	15	38	47	0

The boys, we can see, are much more likely than the girls to use non-standard local pronunciations.

In different parts of the English-speaking world, then, as well as in Koasati, female speakers have been found to use forms considered to be 'better' or more 'correct' than those used by men. Why should this be? As far as English-speaking societies are concerned, we can make intelligent guesses along the following lines. Sociological studies have demonstrated that women in our society are, generally speaking, more status-conscious than men. For this reason, they will be more sensitive to the social significance of social-class-related linguistic variables such as multiple negation. Secondly, it seems that working-class speech, like certain other aspects of working-class culture in our society, has connotations of or associations with masculinity, which may lead men to be more favourably disposed to non-standard linguistic forms than women. This, in turn, may be because working-class speech is associated with the 'toughness' traditionally supposed to be characteristic of working-class life – and 'toughness' is quite widely considered to be a desirable masculine characteristic. We are therefore able to explain the sex differentiation of linguistic variables in English in the following way. Given that there are linguistic variables which are involved, in a speech community, in co-variation with social class (higher-class forms being more statusful or 'correct' than lower-class forms), then there are social pressures on speakers to acquire prestige or to appear 'correct' by employing the higher-class forms. Other things being equal, however, these pressures will be stronger on women, because of their greater status-consciousness. On the other hand, there will also be pressures, as we saw in the case of Martha's Vineyard, to continue using less prestigious non-standard variants as a signal of group solidarity and personal identity. These pressures, however, will be stronger on men than on women, because of concepts of masculinity current in our society. Men's speech will therefore be less 'correct' than that of women.

The point about 'masculinity' is probably the more important, and in a sense it answers the question we posed at the beginning of this chapter. Linguistic sex varieties arise because, as we have already seen, language, as a social phenomenon, is closely related to social attitudes. Men and women are socially different in that society lays down different social roles for them and expects different behaviour patterns from them. Language simply reflects this social fact. Men and women's speech, as we have demonstrated, is not only different: women's speech is also (socially) 'better' than men's speech. This is a reflection of the fact that, generally speaking, more 'correct' social behaviour is expected of women. As a woman interviewed in a Norwegian dialect survey said, when asked why she used the prestige pronunciation [ɛg] 'egg' while her brothers said [æg]: 'It isn't *done* for a woman to say [æg].'

What is more, it seems that the larger and more inflexible the difference between the social roles of men and women in a particular community, the larger and more rigid the linguistic differences tend to be. Our English examples have all consisted of *tendencies* for women to use more 'correct' forms than men. The examples of *distinct* male and female varieties all came from technologically primitive food-gathering or nomadic communities where sex roles are much more clearly delineated.

Thus geographical, ethnic group, and social-class varieties are, at least partly, the result of social *distance*, while sex varieties are the result of social *difference*. Different social attributes, and different behaviour, is expected from men and women, and sex varieties are a symbol of this fact. Using a female linguistic variety is as much a case of identifying oneself as female, and of behaving 'as a woman should', as is, say, wearing a skirt. What would happen to a man who, in our society, wore a skirt? His fate would be the same as that of Carib men who attempted to use women's language: 'The women have words and phrases which the men never use, *or they would be laughed to scorn.*' And just as English-speaking women may be expected to be more 'correct' than their men, so Koasati women were probably expected to be less aggressive and probably therefore less innovative and more conservative than men: conservative language was a sign of femininity.

As far as English is concerned we have some interesting evidence about the way in which social values and sex roles affect speakers' attitudes towards linguistic variants – and hence their actual usage of these variants. We already have plenty of evidence to show that, in England, standard English and the R P accent have high prestige. (It is well-known, for example, that speakers who are paying considerable attention to their speech will move linguistically in the direction of these statusful varieties.) What, however, of the argument that working-class speech has favourable connotations for male speakers? Can we actually show that this is the case? The argument really hinges on the belief that lower-class, non-standard linguistic varieties also have some kind of 'prestige', and that this is particularly so in the case of men. (We can assume that this is the case: otherwise there would be far more R P and standard English speakers than there in fact are.

But it would be very satisfying to be able to show this.) Labov has called this kind of 'prestige' *covert prestige* because attitudes of this type are not usually overtly expressed, and depart markedly from the mainstream societal values (of schools and other institutions) of which everyone is consciously aware. Favourable words like 'good' and 'nice', for instance, are usually reserved for standard prestige varieties.

One example of the evidence which shows that covert prestige exists is as follows. In the urban dialect survey of Norwich, informants were asked to take part in a 'self-evaluation test', in order to investigate what they *believed* themselves to say as opposed to what they actually did say. In this test, words were read aloud to the informants with two or more different pronunciations. For example:

tune   1. [tjuːn]   2. [tuːn]

(The first variant has a y-glide [j], the second 'toon' does not. Both pronunciations are current in Norwich, the former, being the RP pronunciation, having more prestige than the latter.) The informant was then asked to say, by marking a number on a chart, which of the pronunciations he normally used himself. By comparing the results of this test with the data actually tape-recorded during the interviews, it became possible to note discrepancies between what the informant thought or claimed he said and what he *actually* said. The results for the vowel of *tune*, *student*, *music* etc. were very interesting, and are shown in Table 7. Informants are divided into two groups: those who used 50 per cent or more [j] in their tape-recorded conversations were considered to be [j] glide-users, and those with less than 50 per cent non-users.

Table 7. Self-evaluation of tune *in Norwich*

	% informants		
	glide-use claimed	glide-use not claimed	
actual glide-users	60	40	= 100
actual non-users	16	84	= 100

This table shows that a majority of informants were accurate in their self-reporting. 84 per cent of those who did not use [j] glides in conversation stated that they did not do so, and only 16 per cent of non-users actually claimed to use the more prestigious variant when they did not in fact use it. But notice the glide-users. While 60 per cent of them were accurate in their reporting, as many as 40 per cent of them actually claimed to use the lower-status, *non-prestige* pronunciation [tuːn] even though they *normally* said [tjuːn], as demonstrated by the tape-recordings. We can call these people 'under-reporters' since they claimed to use less statusful variants than they actually used, and the 16 per cent group, who went the other way, 'over-reporters'.

If we now break these scores down by sex, the results are rather revealing. Of the 40 per cent under-reporters, half were men and half women. But of the 16 per cent over-reporters, *all* were women. The figures for the sample as a whole are given in Table 8.

Table 8. Over- and under-reporting of tune *in Norwich*

| | | % informants | |
	total	male	female
over-reporting	13	0	29
under-reporting	7	6	7
accurate	80	94	64

Male informants, we can see, are strikingly more accurate than their female counterparts. The women, we can say, report themselves, in very many cases, as using higher-class variants than they actually do – presumably because they wish they did use them or think they ought to and perhaps, therefore, actually believe that they do. Speakers, that is, report themselves as using the form at which they are aiming and which has favourable connotations for them, rather than the form they actually use. (No *conscious* deceit is involved, it seems.)

Consider, now, the figures in Table 9. This shows the results of the self-evaluation test for the vowel in Norwich English in *ear*, *here*, *idea*. (There are two main variants of this vowel in Norwich: 1. [ɪə], as in RP, and 2. [ɛː], – with the vowel of *care*, so that *ear* and *air*, *here* and *hair* are the same.) This table shows not only that a majority of women reported themselves as using RP [ɪə] when in fact they did *not*, but also that as many as *half* the men went the other way and *under*-reported – they reported themselves as using a *less* statusful, more lower-class form than they normally used. This then provides us with evidence to suggest that male Norwich speakers, at a subconscious level, are very favourably disposed to non-standard, low-status speech forms – so much so, in fact, that they claim to use these forms or hear themselves as using them *even when they do not do so*. A large number of male speakers, it seems, are more concerned with acquiring *covert prestige* than with obtaining social status (as this is more usually defined). For Norwich men (and, we can perhaps assume, for men elsewhere) working-class speech is statusful and prestigious.

Table 9. Over- and under-reporting of ear *in Norwich*

	total	% informants male	female
over-reporting	43	22	68
under-reporting	33	50	14
accurate	23	28	18

The clear contrast with the scores of the women informants underlines this point, and demonstrates that they, on the other hand, (with as many as 68 per cent over-reporting in the case of *ear*-type vowels) are much more favourably disposed to middle-class, RP forms. These different attitudes on the part of men and women explain why the sex differentiation portrayed in the case of Norwich *ng* and the two Detroit variables takes the form it does. Because society evaluates different characteristics differently in the two sexes, covert prestige exerts a more powerful influence on men, and 'normal' prestige on women. The result is the social-class-linked sex accents we have seen portrayed in part above.

In Koasati and, in particular, in Chukchi, we saw that women's speech was more conservative than that of men. Linguistic changes, that is, were led by men, and women followed along later, as it were, if at all. Patterns of a similar kind, albeit of a rather more complex type, are also found in Western communities. It is perhaps dangerous to generalize in view of our still very limited knowledge, but it does seem that, here too, women are more conservative than men. However, this only applies to linguistic changes which are operating in the direction away from the prestige standard – glottal stops for /t/ in English, for example. In those cases where there is some kind of high-status variety or national norm, then changes in the direction of this norm appear to be led more frequently by women – largely, one supposes, because of the importance of 'correctness' as a feminine characteristic. In Hillsboro, North Carolina, for instance, women appear to be in the vanguard of the change from an older prestige norm to a newer one. Whereas educated southern speech of the type formerly considered prestigious in Hillsboro is r-less, women especially are now tending to use the more widespread national prestige norm with postvocalic /r/ in words such as *car* and *cart*. A similar development has taken place in the Larvik area in southern Norway, where linguistic changes are taking place in that forms from the town are spreading out into the countryside and taking over from the lower status, earlier, rural forms. Here again women are leading the way. In many families it is possible to isolate three different stages: fathers in the country districts will be more conservative than their sons, and the sons in turn will be more conservative than their mothers and sisters. Women, for example, are more likely to use the prestige town form [mɛlk] 'milk' than the more typically rural form [mjæɽk], and on the whole appear to be a generation ahead of male speakers. In Norwich, too, the same sort of pattern emerges, with women in the vanguard of changes towards prestige pronunciation. There is, however, one exception in Norwich English where a linguistic change has upset the normal pattern of sex differentiation. The variable involved in this unusual case is the vowel of words such as *top*, *hot*, *dog*. In

Norwich this can have a low back rounded vowel, as in RP [tɒp], or an unrounded vowel, [tɑp]. The figures below show the percentage of unrounded non-RP forms used by different speakers:

	MMC	LMC	UWC	MWC	LWC
Male	1	11	44	64	80
Female	0	1	68	71	83

For the two middle-class groups, as one would expect, male scores are higher (they use more non-prestige forms) than female scores. For the three working-class groups, on the other hand, the scores are consistently the other ('wrong') way round: female scores are higher than male scores. We may explain this in the following way: the vowel of *top* is currently undergoing linguistic change in Norwich: rounded vowels of the RP-type are on the increase, as these age-group figures for percentage of unrounded vowels show.

age-group	%
10–29	55
30–49	63
50–69	67
70+	93

The change, however, is taking place in an interesting and unusual way. The newer, rounded vowel is being introduced into Norwich English from RP by middle-class women who are favourably disposed to prestige forms and therefore use nearly 100 per cent of rounded vowels. It is also being introduced, however, by working-class men, in imitation of the working-class speech of the Home Counties and the neighbouring county of Suffolk. These working-class accents, which also use [ɒ], have favourable connotations (covert prestige) for Norwich men, and they therefore use more rounded vowels and have lower scores than working-class women. This, then, is an unusual case of overt prestige and covert prestige coinciding, and it illustrates the role that sex differentiation can play in linguistic change. Men tend to be the innovators, except where changes are taking place in the direction of the standard norm, in which case women tend to be in the vanguard. (This is presumably not inevitable. In a society where men were expected to behave more 'correctly' than women, the linguistic situation would be reversed.)

Sex varieties, then, are the result of different social attitudes towards the behaviour of men and women, and of the attitudes men and women themselves consequently have to language as a social symbol. These attitudes, it is perhaps worth noting, may be of particular importance in an educational situation. In the West Indies, for example, it has been found that children begin to acquire sex-bound attitudes towards standard English as early as the age of six or seven. In a study of children who were native speakers of English Creole (see Chapter 7) learning standard English it was found that, although there were no sex differences in their speech to begin with, after six months of learning, the girls' speech had changed more extensively towards the prestige norm they were being taught than that of the boys – although both had changed to some extent. At the end of the six-month period, for example, boys were using 29 per cent non-standard verb-phrases, while girls were using only $7\frac{1}{2}$ per cent. It was also noticed that, when they thought they were not being observed, some of the boys enjoyed themselves by mimicking, in girlish voices, some of the standard forms that they had learnt. They associated standard speech with femininity, and their motivation to learn was presumably, therefore, that much weaker than the girls'. (This represents, of course, the other side of the 'covert prestige' coin.) Teachers, one would think, cannot afford to ignore this kind of attitude, any more than they can ignore the group-identification function of non-standard speech that we discussed in the previous chapter. Men and women speak as they do because they feel a particular kind of language to be appropriate to their sex. This kind of appropriateness is reinforced by various social pressures: people using inappropriate linguistic behaviour may be rewarded by being 'laughed to scorn', as with Caribs, or, perhaps, even by being put to death, as, reportedly, with the Zulus. In other cases the people concerned may themselves feel uncomfortable, like the West Indian boys, and compensate for this through jokes and mimicking.

In the next chapter we shall discuss the notion of appropriateness at greater length by looking at the linguistic forms considered appropriate to different situations within particular communities.

5. Language and Context

Language, like other forms of social activity, has to be appropriate to the speaker using it. This is why, in many communities, men and women's speech is different. In certain societies, as we have seen, a man might be laughed to scorn if he used language inappropriate to his sex – just as he would be if, in our society, he were to wear a skirt. This, however, is only a part of the overall picture. Behaviour does not only have to be appropriate to the individual, it also needs to be suitable for particular occasions and situations. There are, for example, some circumstances in which a woman who wore a skirt would also be in danger of being laughed at. (A woman competing in a sprint race or going for a swim in a skirt would undoubtedly look somewhat incongruous, to the point of inviting laughter.) This, too, has its counterpart in language. To give a boxing commentary in the language of the Bible or a parish-church sermon in legal language would be either a bad mistake, or a joke. Language, in other words, varies not only according to the social characteristics of the speaker (such as his social class, ethnic group, age and sex) but also according to the social context in which he finds himself. The same speaker uses different linguistic varieties in different situations and for different purposes. The totality of linguistic varieties used in this way – and they may be very many – by a particular community of speakers can be called that linguistic community's *verbal repertoire*.

Many social factors can come into play in controlling which variety from this verbal repertoire is actually to be used on a particular occasion. For example, if a speaker is talking to the people he works with about their work, his language is likely to be rather different from that he will use, say, at home with his family. The *occupational situation* will produce a distinct linguistic variety. Occupational linguistic varieties of this sort have been termed *registers*, and are likely to occur in any situation involving members of a particular profession or occupation. The language of law, for example, is different from the language of medicine, which in turn is different from the language of engineering – and so on. Registers are usually characterized solely by vocabulary differences: either by the use of particular words, or by the use of words in a particular sense. For example, bus-company employees, at least in certain parts of Britain, are much more likely to call buses with two decks *deckers*, while laymen will generally refer to them as *double-deckers*. Similarly, professional soccer players and laymen both discuss football. The footballers, however, are much more likely, in Britain, to refer to the playing area as *the park* than laymen, who are probably more likely to call it *the pitch* (except in areas where *park* is the local-dialect counterpart to *field*). Many other examples of the same sort of phenomena could be cited.

Registers are simply a rather special case of a particular kind of language being produced by the social situation. Many other factors connected with the situation in which language is being used, over and above occupation, will also have a linguistic effect. Language varies, for example, according to whether it is written or spoken. Other things being equal, written English is more formal than spoken English, and the same sort of differences occur in other languages. In French the simple preterite (past historic) tense, as in *il donna* 'he gave', is used in even the most popular detective fiction, but never occurs in speech, where the perfect form *il a donné* is used instead. In some languages the differences may be much greater. In Tamil and in other Indian languages there is a clear and rather considerable difference between a literary variety of the language and a colloquial variety. (This means that, as in the case of some other languages we shall be discussing below, writing is an art which takes many years of formal education to acquire.)

Similarly, the kind of subject matter that is under discussion will have an effect, in addition to that of register, on the language produced. Topics such as molecular biology or international economics are likely to produce linguistic varieties which are more formal than those used in the discussion of knitting or roller-skating. The physical setting and occasion of the language activity will also have some consequences. For instance, academic lectures and ceremonial occasions are more likely to select relatively formal language than, say, public-house arguments, or family breakfasts.

A further important feature of the social context is the 'context' of the person spoken to, and in particular the role relationships and relative statuses of the participants in a discourse. For example, speech between individuals of unequal rank (due to status in an organization, social class, age, or some other factor) is likely to be less relaxed and more formal than that between equals, and in certain languages definite rules may exist as to which linguistic forms may or may not be used. A good example of this is the different forms of *address* that are produced by different degrees of status difference or intimacy. Different degrees of politeness and deference may be required, and these are signalled linguistically. The connotations of English address-forms such as *sir, Mr Smith, Smith, Frederick, Fred, mate* and so on, are all different. Each has different stylistic implications, and the rules for their usage, as well as the frequency of their usage, are quite complex. These rules often vary from class to class, age-group to age-group, and place to place. (There are notable differences between the usage of British and American speakers of English, for example: the term *sir*, for instance, is probably more frequently used in the United States than in Britain.) In some cases there may be considerable uncertainty as to which form is the appropriate one to use – many British people are not certain as to what they should call their parents-in-law, for example – and this may well result in no address-form being used at all. In languages other than English the position may also be complicated by the problem of personal pronoun selection. Most European languages, for instance, unlike English which has only *you*, distinguish, especially in the singular, between a polite and a familiar second-person pronoun:

	familiar	polite
French	*tu*	*vous*
Italian	*tu*	*Lei*
Spanish	*tú*	*usted*
German	*du*	*Sie*
Dutch	*jij*	*u*
Swedish	*du*	*ni*
Norwegian	*du*	*De*
Greek	*esi*	*esis*
Russian	*ty*	*vy*

Originally, it seems, the familiar pronouns were the normal form of address for single individuals, and the polite forms either second-person plural or third-person pronouns (Stage 1 – see p. 107). However, the habit grew up amongst the upper classes in medieval times of showing respect for a person addressed by calling him by what are now the polite pronouns – (following the French forms, we can refer to the familiar pronouns collectively as T, the polite forms as V). This aristocratic habit led to a situation where, although the upper classes called each other V and the lower classes used T amongst themselves, the upper classes used T to the lower-classes who, on the other hand, called them V (Stage 2). This can be interpreted as signifying that where a difference of *power* was involved (the aristocracy having power in the community) in a meeting between two individuals, then pronoun usage was *non-reciprocal*: those with power used T to those without, but received V back, much as a schoolteacher today may call a child *Johnny* but be called *Mr Smith* in return. Subsequently, however, another feature of the social relationship began to have some influence on pronoun selection. Following Roger Brown and Albert Gilman, who have carried out valuable research into T- and V-usage which we shall discuss below, we can call this factor *solidarity*. It seems that the usage of V, which when employed by the power-less to the power-ful signified a difference of power, became generalized to symbolize *all* types of social difference and distance. As a result of this new factor, T-usage now became more probable when the degree of intimacy, similarity or solidarity between speakers was felt to be quite large. This meant that, while the non-reciprocal T–V-usage remained in discourse between unequals, equals now addressed each other as *either T or V*, depending on the degree of intimacy or solidarity involved (Stage 3). In two cases this led to a conflict. Where someone of high rank addressed someone of low rank with whom he was not intimate, such as, for instance, a customer addressing a waiter, then the power factor would suggest T, but the new solidarity factor V. And where a person of inferior rank addressed a superior with whom he *was* intimate, such as a child addressing a parent, then the power factor would indicate V, but the solidarity factor T. In both these cases, in most European languages, the solidarity factor has now won over the power factor, so that pronoun usage is nearly always reciprocal. Instead, for example, of an officer calling a soldier T but receiving V, both now use V, because the relationship, in both directions, is not one of solidarity. And instead of an older brother calling a younger brother T but receiving V, both now use T (Stage 4).

	Stage 1		Stage 2		Stage 3		Stage 4	
	S	NS	S	NS	S	NS	S	NS
a) +P → +P	T	T	V	V	T	V	T	V
b) −P → −P	T	T	T	T	T	V	T	V
c) +P → −P	T	T	T	T	T	*T*	T	V
d) −P → +P	T	T	V	V	*V*	V	T	V

P = power   S = solidarity   NS = no solidarity

Stage 1: original situation, only singular and plural distinguished.

Stage 2: introduction of the power factor, non-reciprocal usage between c) and d).

Stage 3: introduction of the solidarity factor, points of conflict of the two factors italicized.

Stage 4: resolution today of the conflict in favour of the solidarity factor.

Solidarity, presumably because of the gradual rise of democratic egalitarian ideology, has today become the major factor involved. There are still, however, some interesting differences between language communities in T- and V-usage. Brown and Gilman have investigated the extent of T- and V-usage by students from different European and other countries. They found that relationships such as father–son, customer–waiter, boss–clerk were never 'power coded' in modern French, German or Italian. Pronoun-usage was now always reciprocal, although formerly this would not have been the case. Afrikaans speakers, on the other hand, *did* make several non-reciprocal power-coded distinctions in these situations. This, according to Brown and Gilman, signifies a 'less developed egalitarian ethic' on the part of Afrikaans speakers. From their work and from other sources, it also appears that French and Italian speakers are more likely to use T to acquaintances than German speakers; that German speakers are more likely to use T to distant relations; Norwegian schoolchildren are more likely than Dutch or German pupils to use T to their teachers; male Italians are more likely to use T to female fellow students; and that, generally, Italians use more T than the French, who in turn use more T than the Germans. Similar differences were noted by Brown and Gilman between individuals: other things being equal, politically more conservative speakers tended to use fewer T forms than others.

In other linguistic communities further complications arise, since it is not only names or address pronouns that are involved. In both Japanese and Korean, for example, the context of the person addressed can, in addition to particular address-forms, produce rather considerable grammatical and lexical variation as well, depending on the relationship between and the relative statuses of the two people involved. A Korean speaker, for instance, may have to choose one out of six different verb suffixes, depending on his relationship to the person addressed. Unlike English address-forms, moreover, the issue cannot be evaded by 'no-naming' or not selecting an alternative, since verbs may, grammatically, *require* suffixes. In fact, verb forms in Korean may have one of the following suffixes attached to them:

intimate: *-na*
familiar: *-e*
plain: *-ta*
polite: *-e yo*
deferential: *-supnita*
authoritative: *-so*

In other languages restrictions on linguistic forms according to the context of the person addressed may go even further than this. In Javanese, for example, there are several distinct speech 'levels', or varieties which are used in different situations, which involve not only minor differences of pronouns and suffixes but also numerous lexical differences. The levels are relatively discrete, and have names that are well-known in the community. Co-occurrence restrictions also occur at each level: given that a word which belongs to a particular speech level occurs, then only other words from the same level may follow. As with European T and V pronouns, the use of a particular level depends both on the familiarity of the speakers and on their relative statuses. Very often, moreover, the usage is not reciprocal. As an example of the nature of the differences involved, we can cite three different levels of the 'same' sentence as described by Clifford Geertz. These levels all occur in the slightly educated form of a town dialect of Javanese:

'Are you going to eat rice and cassava now?'
1. *Menapa pandjenengan badé dahar sekul kalijan kaspé samenika.*
2. *Napa sampéjan adjeng neda sekul lan kaspé suniki.*
3. *Apa kowé arep mangan sega lan kaspé saiki.*

1 is the high (formal) level and 3 the low (informal) level. Only the word *kaspé* is common to all three levels, although two others occur at two levels and some words appear to be related to each other.

Many aspects of the social situation, then, can contribute to deciding which linguistic variety is to be employed on a particular occasion. Linguistic varieties of this type can be referred to as different *styles*. The styles which make up the verbal repertoire of a particular speaker, therefore, are the particular versions of his dialect which he uses in particular contexts. Very often, as has already been illustrated, these styles can be sited along a scale ranging from informal to formal. Pronouns of the V type signal a relatively formal style, as do the Javanese high level and the Korean polite suffixes. 'Formality' is not, in fact, something which it is easy to define with any degree of precision, largely because it subsumes very many factors including familiarity, kinship-relationship, politeness, seriousness, and so on, but most people have a good idea of the relative formality and informality of particular linguistic variants in their own language. It is not difficult, for example, to decide upon the relative formality of the following pairs of sentences:

I require your attendance to be punctual.
I want you to come on time.

Father was somewhat fatigued after his lengthy journey.
Dad was pretty tired after his long trip.

A not inconsiderable amount of time was expended on the task.
The job took a long time.

Styles of this type in English are characterized by vocabulary differences (*tired* as opposed to *fatigued*; *trip* as opposed to *journey*) but also, as the last pair of sentences shows, by syntactic differences – the passive voice is much more frequent in formal styles in English. These styles resemble the levels of Javanese, which are also signalled by vocabulary differences, but the parallel is not complete, since the same sort of strict co-occurrence restrictions do not operate in English. It is quite possible, for instance, to say:

Dad was pretty fatigued after his long trip.

Another important aspect of situational variation in English is that, as in other languages, not only grammar and vocabulary are involved. As many English speakers shift, according to situation, along the scale of formality, their *pronunciation* changes as well. The actual nature of these 'phonological styles' is rather interesting. The urban dialect surveys of English that we have already discussed (p. 38ff.) were concerned, amongst other things, to relate linguistic variables to the social characteristics of the speaker. They were also, however, interested in the relationship between these variables and social context. It was known, of course, that speakers change their pronunciation from situation to situation (most people know someone who has a 'telephone voice', for example) but there were problems as to how to investigate what form this change took. One obvious difficulty was that, since the data obtained in these surveys was elicited by means of an interview, the style of pronunciation used by informants was largely that variety appropriate to *a tape-recorded interview with a stranger*. The style of speech recorded was, therefore, rather formal compared to everyday conversation. In his New York study, however, Labov overcame this problem and his methodology has subsequently been followed by others. By using, as a controlling factor, the amount of attention paid to speech at any time during the interview, he found that it was possible to produce the equivalent of distinct contextual styles of pronunciation. The main body of conversation obtained in the interviews, because of the artificiality and formality of the situation, contained speech that had more attention directed towards it by the speaker than is normal in everyday speech with close acquaintances. Informants knew their speech was being studied, and were therefore 'on their guard' as far as their pronunciation was concerned. This style of pronunciation has therefore been termed *formal speech*. In certain parts of the interview, however, attempts were made to elicit other styles. At one point, for example, the formality of style was increased by asking the informants to read aloud from a specially prepared reading passage. This produced a style that was even more formal, because reading aloud is a special case, as it were, of written rather than spoken language and, secondly, because reading is a specialized linguistic activity where the speaker pays considerable attention to the way he is speaking. Then the informant also read aloud from a list of individual words. Here the pronunciation was a degree more formal again, since the attention of the reader was concentrated on a single word at a time, a much simpler reading task. In this way, then, three different formal styles of pronunciation were obtained.

What, however, of 'normal', informal speech? Attempts were made to elicit, in spite of the artificial interview situation, normal casual speech such as the informant would use in everyday conversation with his friends and family. Several ways emerged in which this could be done. Casual speech might occur, in the first place, outside the context of the interview, as in conversation with other members of the family who might be present, or in breaks for a coffee or beer. And it was also found that certain questions asked during the interview itself were likely to produce casual speech as a response. Labov, for example, asked his informants if they had ever been in a situation where they thought they were in danger of being killed. Generally informants who related such an incident became emotionally involved in the narrative and, in attempting to convince the interviewer of the reality of the danger, forgot the formal constraints of the interview situation.

In this way four different styles of pronunciation were obtained ranging from the informal, casual speech, through formal speech and reading-passage style, to the most formal, word-list style. This means that scores obtained by informants for particular linguistic variables can be related to interview style and so, by implication, to social context, as well as to social class. We saw earlier how usage of the -ing variable in Norwich English was clearly related to social class. We can now supplement this information with data on stylistic variation as well. Table 10 shows the percentage of non-RP -in' endings used in words like *walking* and *hoping* by the five social classes in the four contextual styles:

Table 10. -in' forms used in four contextual styles in Norwich

	WLS	RPS	FS	CS
MMC	0%	0%	3%	28%
LMC	0	10	15	42
UWC	5	15	74	87
MWC	23	44	88	95
LWC	29	66	98	100

word-list style (WLS); reading-passage style (RPS); formal speech (FS); and casual speech (CS). The twenty scores shown there form a perfect pattern. Scores rise consistently from WLS to CS, and from MMC to LMC, and range from 0 per cent, signifying consistent use of -*ing*, to 100 per cent, signifying, on the part of the LWC in CS, consistent use of -*in*'. This indicates that, just as in more formal contexts speakers are more likely to use words such as *fatigued*, and grammatical features such as the passive voice, so speakers of all classes increase the percentage of high-status RP -*ing* forms in their speech, in the same contexts. It is interesting to note that, although the different social class groups have different levels of -*ing* usage, their evaluation of the two variants is exactly the same. All classes change their pronunciation in exactly the same direction so that, for example, the MMC in their everyday conversation use, on average, the same amount of non-RP forms as the LWC do in their most formal style. In some cases this shifting – with lower classes using, in formal styles, speech characteristics of higher classes in informal speech – can have interesting effects. We have already noted the different percentages of postvocalic /r/ used by speakers from different social-class backgrounds in New York. Figure 4 shows that the overall pattern of class and style differentiation for /r/ follows the same outline as the Norwich -*ing* scores, *except at one point*. The figure shows a steady rise in the use of prestige forms as formality of style increases, so that in formal styles lower-class speech approaches higher-class informal speech. The one exception is, as shown in the cross-over pattern, that the LMC in WLS uses more /r/ than the highest class. In this style the normal pattern of class differentiation is upset. In trying to achieve the prestige style of pronunciation used by the highest class, we can say, the LMC, in the style where most attention is paid to speech, go beyond this level – they overdo it. This kind of linguistic behaviour on the part of the LMC suggests that they are, as the *second* highest class, linguistically and presumably socially somewhat insecure. Because of this linguistic insecurity they pay more attention to speech than other classes, and the degree of style-shifting amongst this group is therefore greater than amongst

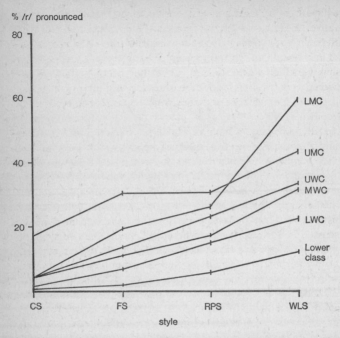

Figure 4. Social-class and style differentiation of postvocalic /r/ in New York City (after Labov)

other classes. This suggests, further, that this particular social group may be instrumental in introducing prestige features such as postvocalic /r/ into particular dialects. Prestige features appear to have more importance for them than for other class groups, and it therefore seems probable that they lead the way in introducing forms of this type to the rest of the community, more so than the highest class.

Thus, in most if not all linguistic communities, differences in social context (broadly defined to include the hearer, the subject matter and the medium as well as the situation) lead to the use of different styles. These styles may be relatively discrete, as appears to be the case in Javanese, or not – the English phonological styles we have just discussed are clearly not distinct, comprising merely relative percentages. These styles can be characterized through differences in vocabulary. including address-forms and pronouns, and in grammar and pronunciation. We can regard these styles as being varieties within dialects, since they occur, within an individual's speech, as a result of features of the social context, and still show characteristics of the speaker's regional and social background.

In all the cases we have noted so far, speakers either move along a scale of formality of style, according to situation, or switch from one separate style of a dialect to another – the situational varieties or styles are clearly sub-varieties of one regional and/or social dialect. Elsewhere, however, situational switching may take place *between* different dialects. (Here we must bear in mind the concepts of discreteness and continuity we discussed in Chapter 1 – the difference between the two types of switching is more one of degree than of kind.) In these cases, one dialect will occur in formal situations, and another in informal situations. For example, native speakers of Lowland Scots dialects may switch, in relatively formal situations, to standard English (spoken with a Scots accent, of course). It is legitimate to regard this situation as rather different from that of an English speaker from England who simply switches styles. In the first place, the difference between the linguistic varieties involved in the switching is much greater. Secondly, as in the case of levels in Javanese, co-occurrence restrictions are involved: it is not usual to use Lowland Scots forms when speaking standard English, or vice versa. And thirdly, whereas other English speakers switch from one variety of their vernacular to another, Scots dialect speakers switch from their own vernacular to that of others – a linguistic variety that they normally learn only at school. (There are clear parallels here with the educational problems faced by lower-class Negro children in America. In both cases, dialect-switching rather than style-switching is required of children in school.)

We can also, at this point, introduce a further reinterpretation of the work of Bernstein (see p. 51). Those children who, according to Bernstein, do not have access to the 'elaborated code', are *not* faced by a dialect-switching problem. The vernaculars of these working-class children, perhaps, simply do not comprise so many *styles* as those of middle-class children. If they are to acquire 'elaborated code', they have to learn new stylistic variants, not a whole new dialect. If this is so, then although it may be true that the children of some working-class Londoners face a language problem when they go to school, their problem cannot be of the same order as that confronting lower-class Negroes or Scots dialect speakers. There is probably no question, in the case of many Scots speakers, of being able to shift along a scale of formality. Rather, they will have to switch over in formal situations to a similar but nevertheless completely distinct variety. The jump from, for example, Scots dialect:

> [av kɛnt jon man eçt jirz]
> *I've kenned yon man eight years.*

to standard Scots English:

> [av non ðat man et jirz]
> *I've known that man eight years.*

is quite considerable, and requires (a) the learning of new words, in this case *know*; (b) the learning of new pronunciations, such as [et]; and (c) the replacement of one known word by another: *yon* becomes *that*. The differences between the style-switching of a Londoner and that of a Scots dialect speaker, simply as far as pronunciation is concerned, are notable:

	informal	formal	informal	formal
one	[jɪn]	[wʌn]	[wʌn]	[wʌn]
two	[twɔ]	[tʉ]	[tʉ:]	[tʉ:]
three	[θri]	[θri]	[fɹi:]	[θɹi:]
eight	[eçt]	[et]	[æɪt]	[ɛɪt]
	A SCOTS DIALECT		A LONDON ACCENT	

In other parts of the world, dialect-switching of the Lowland-Scots–standard-English type may take on a rather different form. In some communities, for example, switching is carried out on a much larger and more institutionalized scale. This sociolinguistic situation has been called *diglossia*. *Diglossia* is a particular kind of language standardization where two distinct varieties of a language exist side by side *throughout* the speech community (not just in the case of a particular group of speakers, such as Scots or Negroes) and where each of the two varieties is assigned a definite social function. (Since the term *diglossia* was first introduced by Charles Ferguson, it has been extended by some writers to include any situation where variety-switching takes place, but I prefer to retain the insights concerning the rather special nature of the situations indicated by the original use, and use the term as just defined.) The two linguistic varieties in a diglossic situation are considered by speakers to be discrete, although this is usually not altogether the case in practice, and comprise a standardized *high* variety and a *low* variety which is also standardized but may be subject to geographical differentiation. The two varieties have overt recognition in the community, and have commonly known and used labels. Examples of language communities which are diglossic, together with the names used, are the following:

	High	*Low*
Swiss German:	Hochdeutsch	Schweizerdeutsch
Arabic:	classical	colloquial
Greek:	Katharevousa	Dhimotiki
Tamil:	literary	colloquial

The most important feature of the diglossic situation is probably the specialization of function of the two varieties. This varies from community to community, but typically the high variety is used in sermons, formal letters, political speeches, university lectures, news broadcasts, newspaper editorials, and 'high' poetry. The low variety, on the other hand, is used in conversation with family and friends, radio serials, political and academic discussions, political cartoons, and 'folk' literature. At other points the linguistic communities vary: most Greeks would probably write a personal letter in the low variety, most Swiss Germans in the high.

The main differences between diglossic and other situations, then, are that the low diglossic variety is standardized, to varying extents (Schweizerdeutsch, Dhimotiki and regional colloquial Arabic are all used on the radio, for instance, although Schweizerdeutsch is not normally written); that the two varieties have names and are felt to be distinct; that the situations where each is to be used are socially fairly well defined; and – and this is of great importance – no section of the community regularly uses the high variety as the normal medium of everyday conversation (this distinguishes it from the English situation, for instance). The high variety has in all cases to be learnt as a school language. This is why the situations where the high variety is used involve either written language or, if spoken language is involved, are situations where preparation is possible. (It has been observed, for example, that an interviewer on Greek television will introduce a guest and conduct the opening pleasantries in Katharevousa, but gradually, and often unwillingly it seems, slip into Dhimotiki as the interview progresses.) Where, in isolated cases, individuals do attempt to use the high variety in everyday speech this is generally felt to be artificial, pedantic, snobbish or reactionary. In German Switzerland it may also be felt to be disloyal, since the high variety, standard German, *is* used as the medium of everyday conversation by speakers *outside* Switzerland.

Generally speaking, the high variety has greater prestige than the low, and is often regarded as more beautiful, even if it is less intelligible. In Arabic and Greek, both of which possess a lengthy literary tradition where the ancient or classical overshadows the modern, it may even be considered good form to write an editorial or poem containing rare or old-fashioned expressions which no one can understand without consulting a dictionary. The use of the two varieties may also be closely linked to religious beliefs and attitudes. There was serious rioting in Greece, for example, when, in 1903, the New Testament was translated into Dhimotiki. Greece is also notable for the political sentiments which are associated with support for either one of the two varieties. Attempts have been made, for instance, to solve the problem of having two standard languages in one nation by establishing a single standard based on the low variety. The particular form of Dhimotiki selected for this role by its adherents is in some ways a mixed language, with considerable admixture from Katharevousa, but Dhimotiki of all types has in any case a very considerable body of literature written in it, and possesses as well several grammars and reference books. Under the Liberal Greek government of the 1960s, this form of Dhimotiki was made the language of schools, and was also used to a certain extent in newspapers. However, since the military coup in 1967, there has been a return, by government decree, to Katharevousa in the schools. Linguistically and educationally this is undoubtedly a retrograde step. It has had the effect of, once again, putting considerable difficulties in the way of children who are learning to read and write. Katharevousa is heavily influenced by older forms of the language and is far removed from the everyday Greek used in speech. In effect, then, this move puts *all* Greek children in a rather worse position than black American speakers of black English vernacular. If they wish to learn to read and write they have first to learn what is in effect a different language. This means that, since the written language is now so distant from the vernacular, only those children whose parents can afford for them to spend many years at school are able to benefit. (In contrast to the Greek government, which has artificially recreated the problem for ideological reasons, the American government is spending considerable sums of money on trying to improve precisely this sort of situation, in spite of the fact that it does not have another standard language ready-made to overcome the problem as the Greeks do.)

Linguistically speaking, the differences between the high and low varieties in the diglossic situation may be considerable. Many of the differences are vocabulary differences: many pairs of words may occur, referring to common objects or concepts, where the meaning is roughly the same, but where the usage of one item rather than another immediately indicates high or low variety. For example, in Arabic the form [raʔaː] *to see* indicates the high classical variety, [šaːf] the low variety. There are generally grammatical differences, too. Many of the differences in Greek, for instance, are morphological, affecting verb and noun endings. The phonology will also often vary. In Greek the two phonologies are quite similar: in Arabic they are different, and in Swiss German very different.

As far as Arabic in general is concerned, the sociolinguistic relationship of the two varieties varies today from country to country. The classical variety is still generally the predominant written language, although colloquial Arabic can now also be written, especially in novels and letters, and there is a tendency for different standards based on regional low varieties to arise in each country. On the other hand, although it is still possible to *speak* the high variety (particularly in lectures, for example) this is increasingly less usual. In normal educated speech there is often a mixture: mainly colloquial Arabic, but with an admixture of classical elements (after the style of the new Greek Dhimotiki). To give some idea of the nature of the linguistic differences involved, we can cite the following examples of some of the contrasts that occurred in a short paragraph of a book written in classical Arabic, together with the colloquial Egyptian equivalents.

	High	*Low*
'I say'	[aquːl]	[aʔuːl]
'I cannot'	[laʔastətiʕ]	[maʔdarš]
'many'	[kaθirah]	[kətir]
'that'	[ðaːkə]	[da]

The diglossic differences between the two types of Arabic can thus be seen to involve the use of different words, together with the substitution of some sounds for others. The following correspondences, for instance, appear to occur in the above examples:

[q] corresponds to [ʔ]
[θ] corresponds to [t]
[ð] corresponds to [d]

The situation in German Switzerland differs somewhat from both the Greek and Arabic situations. Schweizerdeutsch is widely used on Swiss radio, but there is no real agreed standardization. In spite of a tendency to iron out regional differences, as in town speech, many different regional dialects are still widely used by speakers from all social backgrounds. The high variety, standard German, is used, as a spoken language, in parliament, and in courts, churches, universities and the higher forms of schools. It is, however, spoken with Swiss phonology and phonetics, and contains a number of regionalisms (rather in the fashion of standard Scots English), and is therefore markedly different from the spoken standard German of Germany. Otherwise the high variety serves as the *written* language. Children learn to read and write it at school, and, unlike Greek and Arabic, there is no real possibility of writing, say, personal letters in Swiss German dialect. (There *is* a notable body of literature in Schweizerdeutsch, but this is mainly of the somewhat self-conscious dialect-literature type.) Swiss German dialects, on the other hand, are the normal medium of everyday conversation. As an illustration of the nature of the differences involved, we cite the following passage in the low variety, in this case a dialect text based on Zurich speech, with an accompanying equivalent in the high standard German variety. Even from the orthography it can be seen that the phonology is very different, and there are several differences of grammatical construction. There are also some vocabulary differences. *Möödeli*, for example, corresponds to standard German *Gewohnheiten*. Mostly, however, the lexical items in the two passages are related to each other: we can say, for instance, that *tüütsch* and *deutsch* are the 'same word'.

Low Variety – Swiss German:

En Schwyzer isch er zwaar nie woorde, weder en papiirige na äine im Hëërz ine; und eebigs häd mer syner Spraach aagmërkt, das er nüd daa uufgwachsen ischt. Nüd nu s Muul häd de Ussländer verraate, au syni Möödeli. Er häd lieber mit syne tüütsche Landslüüte weder mit de Yhäimische vercheert, und ischt Mitgliid und Zaalmäischter von irem Veräin gsy.

High Variety – Standard German:

Ein Schweizer ist er zwar nie geworden, weder auf dem Papier noch im Herzen; und man hat es seine Sprache angemerkt, dass er nicht dort aufgewachsen ist. Nicht nur die Sprache hat den

Ausländer verraten, sondern auch seine Gewohnheiten. Er hat lieber mit seinen deutschen Landsleuten als mit den Einheimischen verkehrt, und ist Mitglied und Zahlmeister ihres Vereins gewesen.

English:

'He never actually became Swiss, neither on paper nor in his heart; and you could tell from his language that he had not grown up there. It was not only his language that showed that he was a foreigner – his way of life showed it too. He preferred to associate with his German compatriots rather than with the natives, and was a member and the treasurer of their society.'

This gives some indication of the educational problems faced by Swiss German children, who must learn standard German in addition to acquiring literacy. In contrast to the Greek situation, however, where the problem has in a sense been artificially created and where the acquisition of Katharevousa is of no benefit, the acquisition of standard German makes Swiss German children members of the wider German-speaking community, and gives them access to a language of wider communication and to German literature and publications.

A similar situation to that of German Switzerland obtains in Luxemburg. Here too the vernacular of the majority of the inhabitants is a dialect of German. As a focus of national loyalties this dialect has, as a low variety in a diglossic situation, a status far above that of German dialects in Germany. Many Luxemburgers, in fact, consider it to be completely distinct from German, although some of them hesitate to afford it full status as 'a language'. The position in Luxemburg is, however, complicated by the fact that, in addition to the standard German which acts as a high variety, French also plays an important role in Luxemburg society. Luxemburgish is not normally written (although there are some children's books, dialect literature and newspaper articles) and there is no real agreement as to a writing system. Children who have Luxemburgish as their vernacular have to learn to read and write in German when they go to school. Gradually German is also introduced as the *medium* of instruction until, in the last years of school and, often also in higher education, it is replaced by French. This obviously places children in Luxemburg under considerable linguistic strain. On the other hand – again in contrast to the Greek situation – it also means that most educated Luxemburgers are trilingual (at least) and it gives them access to two 'world languages' through which they can gain contact with academic and other literature, and communicate with foreigners when, as many of them do, they travel outside their country. French is the official parliamentary language in Luxemburg, as well as the language of higher education. Public signs and notices tend to be in French; books, newspapers and letters in German; and everyday speech in Luxemburgish. (It is also notable that the Luxemburgish spoken by students tends often to have some admixture of French, rather than of German words.) The following short passage, taken from a newspaper article, illustrates some of the differences between Luxemburgish and standard German as it is used in Luxemburg. These differences, which are lexical, grammatical and phonological, demonstrate the nature of the difficulties faced by Luxemburg children in school:

Luxemburgish:

Wéi de Rodange 1872 sài Buch drécke gelooss huet, du bluf hien drop sëtzen. En hat e puer Leit ze luusség op d'Zéiwe getrëppelt, déi dat net verquësst hun. Eréischt eng Generation doerno huet de Rodange ugefaang séng giedléch Plaz ze kréien. Séng Kanner hu wéinstens nach erlieft, wéi 1927 eng Grimmel vun deem gutt gemaach guf, wat un him verbrach gi wor!

Standard German:

Als Rodange 1872 sein Buch drucken liess, hatte er keinen Erfolg damit. Mit zuviel List war er ein paar Leuten auf die Zehen getreten, und die konnten ihm das nicht verzeihen. Erst eine Generation später begann Rodange, seinen ihm zustehenden Platz zu erhalten. Seine Kinder haben es wenigstens noch erlebt, dass 1927 ein wenig von dem gut gemacht wurde, was an ihm verbrochen worden war!

English:

'When Rodange had his book printed in 1872 he had no success with it. With too much intrigue he had trodden on some people's toes, and they could not forgive him that. Only a generation later did Rodange begin to receive his rightful place. His children at least experienced the making good, in 1927, of some of the wrong that had been done him.'

We have seen, then, that a community's verbal repertoire may encompass simply different styles of the same dialect, as in the case of standard-English speakers; different dialects of the same language, as in the case of Lowland Scots speakers; or, as a special case of the latter, two relatively standardized varieties in a diglossic relationship, as in the case of Arabic. (It is also possible that where, in the diglossic case, the low variety is considerably standardized, the Arabic and Scots situations may be combined: a speaker may switch from local dialect to low standard to high standard, according to the situation.)

In the case of Luxemburg, however, we saw a further complication introduced. Here the diglossic situation is combined with another sociolinguistic activity we can call *language-switching*. So far we have been discussing the way in which speakers switch from one variety to another which is linguistically more or less closely related: formal English, informal English; Scots dialect, standard English; colloquial Arabic, classical Arabic. In many communities, however, the verbal repertoire may contain varieties which are not related; different languages, we can say. As in Luxemburg, where switching occurs between German and French, *language*-switching will take place, like style- or dialect-switching, according to the social situation. (In fact, in some places, all three different types of switching may be involved. The verbal repertoire of many educated speakers in Delhi, for instance, comprises English, a clearly distinct language, as well as Urdu and Hindi, which are considered separate languages but which are very similar, *and* some relatively very different styles of Hindi.)

Paraguay is one of the places where research has been carried out into the nature of language-switching of this sort. Here the two languages involved are Spanish and Guarani, an American Indian language. Guarani has been reported (in the 1960s) as being the vernacular of 88 per cent of the population, approximately, and Spanish of only 6 per cent, but a high percentage know and use both, and both are official languages. Paraguay is unusual in Latin America, since this type of bilingualism has usually indicated a transitional stage leading to Spanish monolingualism. In Paraguay, however, 92 per cent of the population know Guarani, and most speakers continue to use it after learning Spanish. Bilingualism, that is, appears to be a permanent feature of the society. Many features of the social situation seem to be involved in determining which language is to be used. Perhaps the main determinant is the geographical location of a conversation. If this takes place in a rural area, then Guarani is employed. Spanish is not really necessary in the countryside, although it is used in speaking to the village schoolteacher, and is taught and used in school. (Guarani, on the other hand, is not strictly necessary in towns. It is, however, undoubtedly an asset, and anyone unable to speak it would be socially isolated to a certain extent.) In urban areas, though, the position is more complicated. If, for instance, the occasion, or the relationship between the participants, is a *formal* one, then the language used is Spanish. If, however, it is *informal*, then other factors come into play, notably the degree of *intimacy*. If the relationship between speakers is not an intimate one, then Spanish is used (it is said that courting couples begin in Spanish, for example!). But if the relationship *is* an intimate one, then the language used will depend, as in other cases we have already examined, on the topic of conversation. Jokes are always in Guarani, whereas if the topic is a serious one, then the language used will generally be the *mother tongue* (first language learnt) of the speaker concerned (although he will make allowances for the language proficiency of the hearer). Sex may also come into play as a factor here. *Men* for whom Spanish is the first language may still often use Guarani in such situations when speaking to other men. Thus, where in English factors of this sort would produce different styles, in Paraguay they produce different languages.

It is also worth noting that language-switching is not solely *determined* by the social situation. It can also be used by a speaker for his own purposes: to influence or define the situation as he wishes, and to convey nuances of meaning and personal intention. This can be done in one of two ways. It may, for instance, be done by, as it were, using two languages at once. (This is fairly common where a speaker's second language has not been learned through formal education.) For example, in many areas of the south-western USA there are many Mexican-American communities that are bilingual. Their verbal repertoires comprise Spanish and English. The following passage, demonstrating this kind of instant switching, was recorded by John Gumperz and Eduardo Hernandez from a speaker who lives in such a community, and is taken from a discussion on giving up smoking:

I didn't quit, I just stopped. I mean it wasn't an effort I made *que voy a dejar de fumar porque me hace daño o* this or that. I used to pull butts out of the wastepaper basket. I'd get desperate, *y ahi voy al basurero a buscar, a sacar,* you know?

(The two Spanish passages can be translated as: 'that I'm going to stop smoking because it's harmful to me' and 'and there I go to the waste-basket to look for some, to get some'.) This switching, in a culture where English is the dominant language, is presumably subconscious, and has the effect of making the conversation, amongst other things, more intimate and confidential.

The second possibility is that a speaker can switch completely from one language to another. David Parkin has described an interesting example of this from Uganda. Uganda is a multi-lingual country where language-switching takes place according to the social situation but where, as in the Mexican-American example, it can also be used to communicate intentions and nuances over and above the actual verbal message. In Kampala, the capital of Uganda, the sociolinguistic situation is very complex. There are many different ethnic groups living in the town, most of them speaking different languages. Some of the groups are indigenous to Uganda, and others come from Kenya, Sudan and Zaire. In two housing estates which Parkin studied, many different vernaculars are spoken. They include six main groups of *Nilotic* languages; eleven main *Bantu* languages, six of them local and five from eastern Uganda and Kenya; *Arabic*, spoken by Moslems originally from the Sudan; two main groups of *Sudanic* languages; and a small number of speakers of *Nilo-Hamitic* languages. One of the local Bantu languages is *Luganda*. This is the language of the Ganda, who are the ethnic group indigenous to Kampala and are socially dominant in the area. Although most Ganda actually prefer not to live on the housing estates, Luganda is widely understood and spoken by non-Ganda on these estates. Two other languages also play an important role, in spite of the fact that they are not indigenous vernaculars. The people who live on the estates are relatively highly educated, and therefore know and use English, and Swahili is also widely known and used. (Originally Swahili was introduced, for the most part, by Kenyans and Sudan Moslems, but it is now used by many Ugandans, except the Ganda, who tend to see it as undermining their position of dominance.)

This means that many people in Kampala, on these two housing estates and doubtless elsewhere, are often presented with interesting problems of language choice. The position is clearly more complicated than in Paraguay, since many people can speak English, Swahili and Luganda as well as their own vernacular, but the social situation is naturally, once again, a determining factor. Tenants-association meetings, for example, are conducted in English and Luganda in the more prestigious of the two housing estates, and in English and Swahili on the other estate. Language-choice, on the other hand, can also be employed to indicate particular moods and intentions, as we have already seen, and in Kampala the choice is wider than in the Mexican-American communities. For instance, an immigrant from Kenya who was a native speaker of a Bantu language was observed one evening to meet another Kenyan. The second Kenyan was a speaker of an unrelated Nilotic language. They could not, therefore, converse in their vernaculars, but there still remained a choice of which language they should actually use. In fact the selection of a language seems to have depended, as in other cases we have discussed above, on the topic of discussion. The discussion centred round the fact that the first Kenyan had just lost his job, and on, in general, the difficulties facing Kenyans in Uganda. The speakers were, in other words, discussing problems which affected them both. The language they actually used was Swahili. This appears to have been the appropriate language for commiseration, since it was symbolic of their status as equals and of their fraternal relationship. If, on the other hand, the topic had been one involving competition for prestige, such as boasting about money or girls, then they would probably have used English, which would have worked just as well from a purely verbal communication point of view.

Later on the same evening the first Kenyan met a neighbour of his who, although ethnically a Bantu like himself, was a Ugandan, and who held, moreover, a rather senior post. The Kenyan wanted the Ugandan to help him to get a new job, and for this reason he spoke to him in Luganda, since this was the language most appropriate for conveying deference. The Kenyan's Luganda, in fact, was not particularly good, and so the Ugandan changed the conversation over into a third language, English. When, however, the time came for him actually to ask the favour outright, then the Kenyan again switched back to Luganda. In addition to being appropriately deferential, this also had the effect of stressing, since Luganda is a Bantu language, their ethnic affinity, in spite of their different nationalities.

In the next chapter we shall examine multilingual situations of this type in more detail.

6. Language and Nation

At the end of the previous chapter we noted two things about the sociolinguistic situation in Kampala. First, many individuals were either bilingual or multilingual – they could speak more than one language with a fair degree of proficiency. Secondly, this was a consequence of the fact that the society in which they lived was a multilingual society. Individual bilingualism of this type is not actually a *necessary* consequence of societal or national multilingualism: there are multilingual societies where speakers never become bilingual to any significant degree, and individual bilingualism, although much more widespread than the average English speaker might suspect, is by no means universal. But societal multilingualism is a very widespread phenomenon indeed. On a world scale, the multilingual situation that obtains in Uganda is the rule rather than the exception. The vast majority of the nation-states of the world have more than one language spoken indigenously within their frontiers. In some cases, such as Cameroon or Papua, the number of languages may rise into the hundreds (although it is very difficult, bearing in mind the difficulty we mentioned in Chapter 1 of defining what exactly a language is, to give an exact figure for areas like these).

Multilingual nations exist in all parts of the world, and very many examples could be cited. Difficulties only arise when one attempts to locate a country that is genuinely *mono*lingual. There appear to be very few. Even in Europe there are not many true examples, although we are accustomed to thinking of most European nations as monolingual. Most people would accept as true statements to the effect that Germans speak German, Frenchmen speak French, and so on. There are good reasons for this, but the reality of the matter is somewhat different. Nearly all

European countries contain linguistic minorities – groups of speakers who have as their native variety a language other than that which is the official, dominant or major language in the country where they live. In some cases, where the minorities are relatively large, the nation-state usually has more than one official language. Examples are Belgium (Dutch – often known as Flemish in Belgium – and French); Switzerland (German, French, Italian and Romansch); Czechoslovakia (Czech and Slovak); and Yugoslavia (see p. 61). German is also spoken in both Belgium and Czechoslovakia, but does not have national official status in these countries.

Where the minority is smaller or less influential, the minority language or languages are unlikely to have official status, and their speakers, often out of sheer practical necessity, will tend to be bilingual. This last factor is what helps to give Europe its outwardly monolingual appearance. The overwhelming majority of French citizens *can* speak French, in spite of the fact that for a number of them it is a second language. The same sort of situation applies in the United Kingdom. This country also gives every appearance of being monolingual, and visitors certainly need to learn no other language than English. Even this appearance, though, is somewhat deceptive. It is true that England has not had an indigenous linguistic minority since Cornish became extinct in the eighteenth or nineteenth century (accounts vary), but there are today sizeable groups of speakers of languages from the northern Indian subcontinent, such as Punjabi, living in the country (and there are also some grounds for arguing that the first language of many British people of West Indian origin is not English, although it is very similar – see Chapter 7). Welsh, moreover, is the first language of about a quarter of the population of Wales, while Scots Gaelic is spoken natively by about 80,000 people largely in the West Highlands and Hebridean Islands of Scotland (1961 census figures). Irish Gaelic, too, is still spoken by small numbers of speakers in parts of Northern Ireland.

The extent of national multilingualism in Europe is illustrated in the following lists. The first list gives some idea of the extent to which languages that, while dominant official national languages in particular countries, are spoken by linguistic minorities elsewhere. (Languages spoken only in the USSR are not included.)

Language	Spoken by Linguistic Minority in:
German	Denmark, Belgium, France, Italy, Yugoslavia, Rumania, USSR, Hungary, Czechoslovakia, Poland
Turkish	Greece, Yugoslavia, Bulgaria, Rumania, USSR
Greek	Italy, Yugoslavia, Albania, Rumania, USSR
Albanian	Greece, Yugoslavia, Italy
Hungarian	Austria, Yugoslavia, Rumania
Finnish	Sweden, USSR
Swedish	Finland, USSR
French	Italy, Luxemburg
Polish	USSR, Czechoslovakia
Bulgarian	Rumania, USSR
Danish	West Germany
Dutch	France
Russian	Rumania

In addition to these, a number of languages which have official status in certain provinces or parts of particular countries are also minority languages elsewhere.

Language	Official in:	Minority Language in:
Ukrainian	USSR	Rumania, Czechoslovakia
Slovak	Czechoslovakia	Hungary, Rumania
Czech	Czechoslovakia	Poland, Rumania
Slovene	Yugoslavia	Austria, Italy
Serbo-Croat	Yugoslavia	Rumania, Austria
Macedonian	Yugoslavia	Bulgaria, Greece

Finally, there are a number of languages which are everywhere minority languages. Some of these are the following:

Language	Spoken in:
Lappish	Norway, Sweden, Finland, USSR
Frisian	Denmark, Germany, Holland
Basque	Spain, France

Catalan	Spain, France
Breton	France
Sorbian	East Germany
Kashubian	Poland
Welsh	UK
Gaelic	UK

In addition to these, Yiddish and Romany (Gypsy) are quite widely spoken as minority languages in different parts of the continent. (The unusual case of Irish Gaelic will be discussed below.)

So, nearly all European nations are multilingual to a certain extent. Perhaps the most multilingual of all the countries in Europe, apart from the USSR (most of which is in Asia anyway, of course) is Rumania. About 85 per cent of the population have Rumanian as their mother tongue, but at least fourteen other languages are spoken natively in the country. In 1956 the relative proportions of the different language groups, as illustrated by the number of Rumanian citizens who have a particular language as their mother tongue, were approximately as follows:

Rumanian	15,080,600
Hungarian	1,652,700
German	395,400
Ukrainian	68,300
Romany	66,900
Russian	45,000
Serbo-Croat	43,100
Yiddish	34,300
Tartar	20,600
Slovak	18,900
Turkish	14,200
Bulgarian	13,200
Czech	6,200
Greek, Armenian, others, and 'not known'	29,000

Multilingualism on this scale clearly brings problems for governments and others concerned with national organizations of various kinds, and we shall discuss these problems below (pp. 139–56). Multilingualism on any scale, though, also brings with it problems for individuals and groups of individuals, especially those who are members of linguistic minorities. Unlike members of the majority-language group, they have to acquire proficiency in at least two languages before they can function as full members of the national community in which they live. Perhaps the biggest problem they have to face is educational. We have already discussed, in earlier chapters, the educational problems that may be encountered by children who have to learn to read and write in a dialect which is radically different from their own. The problems of children from linguistic minorities who have to learn to read and write in an entirely different language are perhaps of the same type but, obviously, considerably greater. In very many instances in different parts of the world children are faced with precisely this difficulty. In some cases the problem will not, perhaps, be too severe, because the two languages involved may not be particularly different. Frisian children learning Dutch are presented with nothing like the difficulty of Lapp children learning Swedish, since Frisian and Dutch are quite closely related languages. Or it may be that the educational policy of the country concerned is reasonably sophisticated linguistically, and the children learn to read and write in and are taught through the medium of their native language in the initial stages of their schooling, with the majority language being introduced later on. This approach has been adopted in many parts of Wales, as well as in Rumania and many other places. Its aims are that the children should acquire an ability to read, write and speak both their native language and the majority language, and has clear parallels with the *bidialectalism* approach to non-standard dialects of English that we discussed in Chapter 3, pp. 81–2. In both cases the two linguistic varieties involved are considered as respectable linguistic systems in themselves, and the child is encouraged to use both.

In other cases the minority child may be faced with very considerable difficulty. This may occur where the two languages involved are not closely related and also, more importantly, where the educational policy of a particular nation-state is to discourage, or simply to ignore or not to encourage, minority languages. In extreme cases the minority language may be forbidden or disapproved of in school, and children punished or actively discouraged from using it there. This was formerly true both of Welsh in Wales and Gaelic in Scotland – at one time a law was in force that actually made the speaking of Gaelic illegal. This approach to minority languages has distinct parallels with the 'elimination of non-standard speech' approach towards nonstandard dialects discussed earlier. In both cases the language variety to be eliminated or discouraged is regarded as inferior. (This is in all cases a social judgement. 'The Welsh language is inferior to English' has absolutely no basis in *linguistic* fact.) And in both cases the psychological, social and pedagogical consequences are serious. But where Welsh, Gaelic and other minority languages are concerned, the effects of the attempted imposition of an alien standard such as English may be much more serious. The attempted replacement of one language by another entails an effort (which may be well-intentioned of course) to obliterate whole cultures; it is indicative of illogical ethnic attitudes ('The Welsh are inferior to the English'); and it can very seriously impair the educational progress of a child who has to learn a new language before he can understand what the teacher is saying, let alone read and write.

This approach was for many years official policy in the United States, where it may have been at least partly responsible, together with the broader social attitudes to minority languages that went with it, for the widespread and rapid assimilation of minority language groups to the English-speaking majority. Generally, children of parents born outside America who spoke languages such as Chinese, Yiddish, Italian, Greek, Polish, Dutch, Norwegian, Swedish, and many more, have not retained more than a passive knowledge of their parents' languages. Today provision *is* made for some groups, notably Spanish-speakers in the South-West and some American Indians, to be educated in their own language, and certain other steps have also been taken: public notices in New York City, for example, are posted in Spanish as well as English, to cater for the large Puerto Rican community now living there. However, even the larger, more rural linguistic minorities such as those consisting of speakers of French (in the North-East and in Louisiana) and Pennsylvania Dutch (a form of German) are rapidly declining in size. In 1960, the ten largest linguistic minorities in the US were as follows:

Italian	3.7 million	Yiddish	1.0 million
Spanish	3.3	Russian	0.5
German	3.1	Swedish	0.4
Polish	2.1	Hungarian	0.4
French	1.0	Norwegian	0.3

In all, about 20 million Americans currently have a mother-tongue other than English.

Happily, this approach and the attitudes associated with it have almost disappeared from the educational scene in the United Kingdom, although there are still many Welsh and Gaelic speakers who are very unhappy about the status of their languages in this country. Gaelic has been allowed in schools in Gaelic-speaking Scottish areas since 1918, although it was not really until 1958 that it began to be used extensively as a medium of instruction, and then mainly for younger children in primary schools. For most older children, particularly in secondary schools, English is still the normal medium, partly as a consequence of the centralization of secondary education which has meant that many Gaelic speakers go to schools where there are also large numbers of non-Gaelic-speaking children.

The position of Welsh in the UK is considerably more healthy than that of Gaelic. It has far more speakers, and fairly considerable amounts of time are given to radio and TV broadcasts in Welsh (although not as much as some would like). As in the case of Gaelic, the effects of the older educational approach linger on. Many older people today, while being fluent speakers of Welsh, have never learned to write it. They have to write even the most intimate of letters in a foreign language, English, and very often find it difficult to read standard Welsh. Today the situation is much improved, and especially since the early 1930s there has been a change in emphasis. At around that time

Welsh began to be taught seriously in many primary schools in Welsh-speaking areas, although its role in secondary schools was very minor. Subsequently, in 1953, a report was published which received Ministry of Education approval: it suggested that all children in Wales should be taught both Welsh and English. This bilingual policy has been widely adopted today, although the actual situation is rather complex since policy is decided on an area basis by local education authorities. Generally, however, one can say that in most parts of Wales, whether anglicized or not, one can find some schools at both primary and secondary level where Welsh is taught only as a subject, others where it is used as a medium along with English, and others where Welsh is the only medium and English is taught as a subject. Another interesting development is the institution of nursery schools which are solely Welsh-speaking but to which many English-speaking parents are sending their children in order that they should grow up bilingual. Like, apparently, many Irish people, some of these Welsh parents feel that by adopting the English language they or their ancestors have in some way been untrue to their cultural traditions, and hope that their children will be able to rectify this state of affairs. The schools appear to work very well, and suggest that there may well be an increase in the number of fluent Welsh speakers in the next generation. Nevertheless, the future of the Celtic languages in Britain is still very precarious. There has been a decline in the number of Gaelic speakers in Scotland from 136,000 in 1831 to 81,000 in 1931, and a decline in the number of Welsh speakers over the same period from 902,000 to 656,000.

The teaching of minority languages in this way is obviously of benefit to minority-group children, not only in the learning of reading and writing but in other subjects as well. It also has the effect of recognizing the child's social and cultural identity and integrity and encourages the development and growth of minority cultures. At the same time, like the *bidialectalism* approach, it does not deny the child access to the majority language which is likely to be essential for upward social mobility. Gaelic and Welsh speakers who know English can more readily function as members of the wider national community, if they wish to.

The position of other European minority languages in education varies considerably. Those languages, like German, which are majority languages elsewhere have a clear practical advantage over languages like Gaelic and Lappish for which there is a scarcity of teaching materials and reading matter. On the other hand, they may be at a political disadvantage. German receives very little encouragement in France, while Macedonian in Greece and German in Italy are actually discouraged. (We shall discuss this political point below.) Frisian is given some encouragement in Holland, while some attempts have been made to promote Lapp education in Scandinavia, in spite of many parents' objections that their children 'learn Lappish at home'. (Their concern is clearly that their children's language should not be a barrier to their social advancement, and parallels some of the objections to the 'appreciation of dialect differences' approach cited in Chapter 3.)

We have already seen that the other two approaches to non-standard dialects have their parallels in attitudes to linguistic minorities, so what of this third approach, the 'appreciation of dialect differences' – are there any parallels here? In a way, there are. This view states that there is no need for a child to learn a new dialect because there is nothing wrong with the one he already has. To translate this into equivalent, linguistic-minority terms would be to say something like, 'There is no need for Spanish Basques to learn Spanish, because Basque is itself a perfectly good language.' The parallel does not quite work, because clearly there *is* a need for Basques to learn Spanish, since they live in Spain and have to function as part of Spanish society. The argument, therefore, has to be taken one stage further: there would be no need for Basques to learn Spanish *if*, as Basque nationalists advocate, they did not live in Spain, but were given their political independence and could form a nation-state of their own. This is the type of argument that minority groups are able to use in their campaigns for independence. Their solution to the problem is to convert linguistic minorities, through political autonomy, into linguistic majorities. Some governments have responded to this sort of pressure by granting partial independence, as in the establishment of the autonomous Albanian-speaking area of Yugoslavia, and the autonomous Hungarian regions of Yugoslavia and Rumania.

Where language is a defining characteristic (see p. 59) of a minority ethnic group wanting independence, particularly where other (for example physical) characteristics are not significant (as in the case of Welsh), linguistic factors are likely to play an important role in any separatist movement they might undertake. This is partly in response to practical problems, as outlined in the argument above, but mainly a result of the fact that language, as we have already seen (pp. 24, 80), acts as an important symbol of group consciousness and solidarity. The extent to which this is true is revealed in the part played by linguistic groupings in the development of new independent nations in Europe after the breakdown of the older, multilingual empires. As national consciousness grew, languages like Czech, Serbo-Croat and several others, developed a literature, underwent standardization, and emerged as national languages of fairly monoglot areas when independence was achieved.

The rapid increase in the number of independent European nation-states in the past hundred years or so has therefore been paralleled by a rapid growth in the number of autonomous, national, and official languages. During the nineteenth century the number rose from sixteen to thirty, and since that time has risen to over fifty (if we include the USSR). It is interesting to plot some of the stages of this development, particularly since the movement has not been entirely in one direction. During the Middle Ages, for example, some languages – like Provençal and Arabic – ceased to function (the latter in Europe alone) as standardized official languages, while others – like English and Norwegian – became submerged, only to reappear later. By 1800, the following had come to be operating as national languages in Europe (excluding Russia): Icelandic, Swedish, Danish, German, Dutch, English, French, Spanish, Portuguese, Italian, Polish, Hungarian, Greek, and Turkish. By 1900 the following had also made an appearance (or reappearance) as standardized national, official or written languages: Norwegian, Finnish, Welsh,

Rumanian, and the Slav languages Czech, Slovak, Slovene, Serbo-Croat, and Bulgarian. And during the rest of this century Irish Gaelic, Scots Gaelic, Breton, Catalan, Romansch, Albanian and Basque have all undergone revival or expansion. (Ireland, Norway, Czechoslovakia, Yugoslavia and Albania have all achieved independence or nationhood in the present century, and in many cases even where minorities have not won independence, greater recognition has been afforded their languages, as in the case of Gaelic and Welsh.)

The problems of the multilingual situation for the individual, therefore, can be overcome or minimized either through political independence or semi-independence, or, less drastically, through adequate educational programmes and policies. What, however, of the problems of multilingualism for national governments? As we have seen, many governments regard as a problem the fact that language can act as a focus of discontent for minorities wanting more power, independence, or annexation by a neighbouring state. Where governments do not regard this as threatening or undesirable, they may well regard linguistic minorities benevolently (or simply ignore them). It does not appear, for example, that the British government is seriously concerned about Gaelic speakers. (On the other hand, punitive action has on occasions been taken against some Welsh speakers who think that Welsh still has inferior social status and have wished to draw attention to this fact, and it has been reliably reported in recent years that Welsh-speaking people remanded in custody have been forbidden to speak to visitors in their native language – which is in fact a violation of the Declaration of Human Rights.) Scandinavian governments, similarly, clearly believe they have nothing to fear from Lapps. The government of the Republic of Ireland, too, gives active support to the minority language (something between 1 and 3 per cent of the population speak Irish natively), and have made it a compulsory subject in schools. This, of course, is because Irish was formerly the language of all Irishmen and as such symbolizes national culture and identity rather than dissidence of any kind.

On the other hand, in cases where governments regard linguistic minorities as potentially 'subversive', they may react very differently. Their fears, from their own point of view, may often be justified: language loyalty can be a powerful weapon, and has often been manipulated to political advantage. In many cases a repressed or discouraged minority language is also the language of a possibly antagonistic neighbouring state – this has been true of Macedonian in Greece, or German in France and Italy – and the fear is that language loyalty may prove to be stronger than national loyalty. In other cases disfavoured minority languages may simply have acted as catalysts of discontent, because minority groups have had one additional reason to be dissatisfied with their lot.

One language which has had a history of oppression for reasons of this kind is Catalan. Catalan is a Romance language which is about as closely related to French as it is to Spanish. It has approximately seven million speakers in Spain – in Catalonia, Valencia and the Balearic Islands – as well as about 250,000 in Roussillon in France, and a very small group in Sardinia. It was the official, administrative written language in Catalonia until that area was annexed by Castile at the beginning of the eighteenth century. Subsequently, in 1768, Spanish was introduced by government decree into formerly Catalan schools, and then in 1856 a law was passed which stated that all political documents and legal contracts were to be in Spanish. Liberalization of this policy took place under the Spanish Republic, from 1931 to 1939. Catalan-speaking children were taught in Catalan, while provision was made for Spanish-speaking children in the Catalan area to begin their education in Spanish and at the age of ten both groups started to learn the other language as well. However, under the Franco government Catalan was once again banned completely from schools, and chairs of Catalan language and literature at the University of Barcelona were abolished. Catalan text books disappeared, and Catalan children had again to begin and complete their education in Spanish. Supporters of Catalan have claimed that the Franco government is fundamentally 'Castilian nationalist' in character, and clearly it has been concerned about what it has regarded as separatist tendencies. Language is a signal of group identity, and anybody attempting to create a unified nation-state, particularly of the corporate Spanish type, will find any signalling of a *different* identity undesirable or dangerous. Linguistic subjugation (or unification, depending on one's point of view) is therefore an important strategy in implementing political subjugation (or unification).

The position of Catalan today is that the situation is somewhat relaxed. Many books are now available and there are two children's comics and one magazine in the language. There are still, however, no newspapers, and broadcasting time is very limited indeed. Most significant of all is that Catalan remains forbidden in the schools. This means that upon arriving in school for the first time, Catalan children are unable to understand what the teacher is saying – for the first few weeks at least – and that they grow up unable to read and write in their own language, unless their parents take the trouble to teach them these skills at home. The extent of the linguistic problem involved is partly revealed by the following passage in Catalan, and its Spanish translation.

Catalan:

Maigret escolta distret, tot pensant que la meitat de París està de vacances i que la resta, en aquesta hora, beu begudes fresques a les tauletes de les terrasses. Quina comtessa? Ah sí! L'home trist s'explica. Una senyora que ha tingut més d'un revés de fortuna i que ha obert un saló de bridge al carrer Pyramides. Una dona ben bonica. Es nota que el pobre home n'està enamorat. -Avui, a les quatre, he agafat un bitllet de mil de la caixa dels amos.

Spanish:

Maigret escucha distraídemente, pensando que medio París está de vacaciones y que el resto a estas horas estará tomando refrescos en las mesitas de las terrazas. Que condesa? Ah, sí! El hombre triste s'explica. Una señora que ha sufrido más de un contratiempo y que abrió un salón de bridge en la calle Pirámides. Una mujer muy guapa. Se conoce que el pobre hombre está enamorado. -Hoy, a las cuatro, he cogido un billete de mil de la caja de los dueños.

English:

'Maigret only half listens, thinking that half Paris will be on holiday and that the rest, at this hour, will be drinking cool drinks outside at small café-tables on the pavement. Which countess? Ah yes! The sad man explains. A lady who has had more than one set-back and who has opened a bridge-club on Pyramides street. A rather pretty woman. It is apparent that the poor man is in love with her. "Today, at four o'clock, I took a thousand-franc note from the bosses' till."'

The same sort of motives that we have ascribed to the Spanish government were clearly also present in the case of the British government which prohibited Scots Gaelic in the aftermath of the 1745 rebellion. Similar factors have influenced the actions of those anti-communist Greek governments which have carried out a policy of hellenization in northern Greece by proscribing the usage of Macedonian (official in communist Yugoslavia) in that area.

A further example of government intervention in the affairs of linguistic minorities for what are ultimately political purposes comes from the Soviet Union. This country has about 200 different languages spoken within its frontiers. The languages fall linguistically into six main genetic groups. The *Paleoasiatic* languages are spoken mainly in Siberia, many of them by technologically non-advanced groups of nomads or settlers. They are possibly related to Eskimo, and may include Ainu, which is also spoken in Japan. The *Uralic* languages, which are related to Finnish, include Lappish and Estonian, while the *Altaic* languages include Turkish, Manchurian, Mongolian and Tartar. The Soviet Union also has *North Caucasian* and *South Caucasian* languages (including Georgian), and *Indo-European* languages. The latter comprise Armenian, a number of Iranian languages, the Baltic languages Latvian and Lithuanian, the Germanic languages German and Yiddish, and the Slavonic languages Ukrainian, Polish and Byelorussian (White Russian), as well as Russian itself.

After the 1917 revolution Soviet policy was to encourage each ethnic group to develop its own language, and to promote the Latin alphabet as being international. Under Stalin, however, there was a sharp reversal. The policy became one of impressing uniformity on the country, and the status of minority languages was greatly decreased. It was decreed, for example, that all new technical words introduced into minority languages should be borrowed from Russian, and the Latin alphabet was declared to be 'undesirable' (Russian is written in the Cyrillic alphabet). Some languages remained relatively privileged, like Georgian (Stalin's native language) and languages of large or influential groups such as Ukrainian and Armenian, while others, including Yiddish and the Paleoasiatic languages, were very much discouraged. Today, generally speaking, a number of pressures of various types are exercised in favour of Russian and against the maintenance of minority languages. Russian, for example, is officially praised as a 'second native language' and as an 'unfailing source of enrichment' of minority languages. Opposition to the introduction of Russian loan-words or the compulsory study of Russian is labelled 'bourgeois nationalist'. Parents who opt for Russian as the school medium in areas where choice is possible are officially praised, and it is becoming increasingly necessary to know Russian for social advancement. About sixty of the 200-odd languages are actually used in primary education, although this number is falling. (Before the war, for example, twenty-two languages were used in primary education in Uzbekistan, whereas now only seven are employed.) The situation in schools varies from place to place, and may depend on parental choice. Many children *are* taught in their minority language throughout the primary school, but others are not: children who are native speakers of Ossetic (an Iranian language) receive all their education in Russian apart from one hour a week in Ossetic. In secondary schools Russian is widespread, and, apart from Armenian and Georgian, it is universal in higher education, with the exception of a number of language, literature and education faculties. We should also note that factors outside the educational situation can also help to effect linguistic russianization. In Kazakhstan, for instance, only 30 per cent of the population are now native Kazakh speakers, because of the influx of Russian-speaking officials and other immigrants, who generally make no attempt to learn the indigenous language.

In these cases, groups of people have been prevented or discouraged from using their native language for political reasons. Political oppression through language, however, can take a different form, as the situation in South Africa shows. Like the USSR, South Africa is a very multilingual nation. It contains the following language groups:

Bantu languages:

Xhosa	20%	
Zulu	18%	
Sotho	14%	TOTAL 65%
Tswana	5%	
others	8%	

European languages:

Afrikaans ('white' speakers)	11%	
('coloured' speakers)	9%	
English ('white' speakers)	8%	TOTAL 30%
('coloured' speakers)	1%	
Dutch, German	1%	

Indian languages:

Tamil	2%	
Hindi	2%	TOTAL 5%
others	1%	

As is well-known, the ruling Afrikaaner (white Afrikaans-speaking) nationalists in South Africa have imposed a rigid separation on the different ethnic groups within their society. Until quite recently an integral part of this policy was not to suppress the African languages (which are by no means minority languages, as the figures show, but which have clearly depressed status) as in the Soviet Union, but to *encourage* them, and to deny Africans access to Afrikaans and, especially, English. This was part of a policy to retribalize all Africans into separate (and isolated) ethnic groups, a policy which can be interpreted as being part of a 'divide-and-rule' strategy. The Bantu Education

Department had as its stated aim the education of all Africans in their mother tongue. Because this was to be education *in their mother tongue alone*, many of the Africans did not regard this as a valuable democratic right, but rather as an attempt to isolate them from each other, from the ruling elite, from possibilities of advancement, and from international literature and other contacts. (Government policy appears now to have changed, and English and Afrikaans are being more widely taught in African schools.) The relationship between minority language groups and government policy is therefore far from straightforward: identical policies can have different implications in different contexts.

The activities of the governments we have been discussing so far can be described as instances of *language planning*. In very many cases activities of this kind, unlike many of those we have just described, can be regarded as both necessary and commendable – for example in countries which are faced with the problem of having to select a national language or languages and, subsequently, of developing and standardizing it. We have already noted some of the problems resulting from multilingualism in Europe. In many areas of the world the problems are considerably more complex. Sub-Saharan Africa, for example, is a very multilingual area where language problems have been exacerbated because colonial powers have drawn national frontiers without regard for the geographical distribution of ethnic or linguistic groups.

However, communication problems in areas like these are not necessarily so serious as one might think. In our Kampala example, for instance (p. 126), we saw that people were able to communicate with each other quite easily, in spite of the fact that they did not know each other's languages, because they were also familiar with other languages like Luganda, Swahili and English: each of these three languages was capable of functioning as a *lingua franca*. A *lingua franca* is a language which is used as a means of communication among people who have no native language in common. Some of the languages which are used in this way in Africa, like English and French, are not indigenous to the area in question and are often learned through formal education. Many African lingua francas, though, are indigenous, and may have come to be used as such because of the political dominance of Africa's native speakers, like Luganda, or because they were prominent traders in the area, like Swahili. In West Africa one of the most important lingua francas which is still used for predominantly trading purposes is Hausa. Hausa is an Afro-Asiatic language spoken originally in the region of Lake Chad in north-central Africa, but it has become so widely known that it is used for trading and other purposes by many millions of speakers in areas such as Ghana, Nigeria and Dahomey. Many languages have spread as lingua francas in the same kind of way, only to contract again later for reasons of economics or politics. Greek, for example, became a lingua franca in the ancient world as a result, initially, of Alexander's military conquests, and was at one time used widely from Turkey to Portugal. Latin was later used as a lingua franca in the western world, mainly as a result of the expansion of the Roman empire, and later survived as such, in spite of the fact that it had no native speakers, for many centuries. The original 'lingua franca' from which the term (which actually means 'French language') is derived, was a form of Provençal that was used as a lingua franca by the multilingual crusaders.

When governments are presented with the problem, as many 'new' nations have been, of selecting a national language or languages, lingua francas of this type are obviously very useful. There are clear advantages to be gained from the selection of a language which many people already understand. In some cases, though, complications may arise because competing or alternative lingua francas are available. In India, Hindi is used as a lingua franca in much of the northern part of the country. It has the advantage of being an indigenous rather than an originally colonial language, like English, but it also has the disadvantage of benefiting native speakers to the detriment of others who have to learn it as a second language. English, on the other hand, operates as a lingua franca throughout the country, but tends to be used only by relatively educated speakers: an educated Bengali speaker would probably communicate in English with an educated Tamil speaker if, as is likely, neither knew the other's first language.

A similar problem of competing lingua francas has occurred in Malaysia. The Federation of Malaysia was formed in 1963 with a population of only ten million, but with a linguistic situation that was very complex. In Malaya itself Malay is the native language of perhaps 30 per cent of the population, although it has several different forms, including the standard Malay of the educated urban elite; colloquial Malay, which has many different dialectal variants; and 'bazaar Malay' which is widely used as a trading lingua franca. Another 30 per cent speak one of twelve different Chinese languages, the four most widely used being Cantonese, Hokkien, Hakka and Tiechiu. (In each urban Chinese community one of these normally functions as a lingua franca.) Then roughly 10 per cent speak various Indian languages, mainly Tamil, but also other Dravidian languages such as Telugu and Malayalam, and the Indo-European Punjabi, and, in addition to these, many of the Eurasian community speak a form of Portuguese, while English is a lingua franca for many of the educated. Thai and several 'aboriginal' languages are also spoken. The sociolinguistic picture is further complicated by the languages which are used as the medium of instruction in schools. Malay, Tamil and English are all used in this way, but so is Mandarin Chinese, which is not one of the main varieties of Chinese spoken natively in the country, and Arabic. Elsewhere, in those parts of the Federation that formerly constituted British North Borneo, many different languages are spoken which are related to Malay, as well as some that are related to certain of the languages of the Philippines, and also Chinese. There is therefore clearly a problem in Malaysia as to which language should be selected to act as the national language. Malay is the most widely understood lingua franca, but Malays are politically dominant in the country and attempts to make Malay the sole official language might well cause some resentment among the Chinese and Indians. It would also entail a shortage of textbooks, many of which are now in English, and a certain amount of loss of international contacts. English on the other hand cannot be claimed to be in any sense a national language, but it is the most popular educational medium, for what are largely economic reasons. Success in the professions in Malaysia appears to require ability in English, while Malay is required for the Civil Service, and Chinese for business. The problem has as yet not really been solved, but while group identity plays an important part in maintaining language loyalty towards languages like Tamil, these community languages appear to be gradually ceding in importance to Malay (for reasons of national loyalty) and to English (for reasons of international economics) in more official functions and circumstances. Government policy appears to be in the direction of strengthening both Malay and English.

A further solution has sometimes been advocated for problems of multilingualism – that an artificial language such as Esperanto should be adopted as a lingua franca. At present it seems unlikely that any nation-state will adopt Esperanto as its official language because of the practical problems involved, and also because, being a neutral language, it is not national in any way. However, supporters of Esperanto are much more concerned to see it used as a world-wide lingua franca in order to solve problems of *international* multilingualism. In multilingual, multinational communities, like the European Common Market, disputes can often arise as to which language or languages are to be used officially. Advocates of Esperanto would suggest that, if it were made the official language of the Common Market, disputes of this kind would not arise. Unlike English or French, Esperanto is the native language of no one, and therefore gives nobody an unfair advantage, just as English in India is in many ways a fairer choice as a lingua franca than Hindi. This argument would probably not hold, however, for larger international organizations like the United Nations. This is because Esperanto, although it is easier to learn than natural languages, is quite clearly a *European*-type language, and would therefore benefit native speakers of languages originally from this area. In any case, there are as yet no real signs of Esperanto, or any other similar language, making very great headway on the international scene.

Often the role of a national government does not stop at selecting a national language. Once selected, the language may have to be established, developed and standardized. The government, for example, may play a part in developing a suitable orthography, or in deciding whether a particular dialect of the language or some set of compromise forms should be selected. English, of course, developed a standard variety by relatively 'natural' means, over the centuries, out of a kind of consensus, due to various social factors. For many 'newer' countries, though, the development of a standard language has had to take place fairly rapidly, and government intervention has therefore been necessary. Standardization, it is argued, is necessary in order to facilitate communications, to make possible the establishment of an agreed orthography, and to provide a uniform form for school books. (It is, of course, an open question as to how much, if any, standardization is really required. It can be argued quite reasonably that there is no real point in standardizing to the extent where, as is often the case in English-speaking communities, children spend many hours learning to spell in an *exactly* uniform manner, where any spelling mistake is the subject of opprobrium or ridicule, and where deviations from the standard are interpreted as incontrovertible evidence of ignorance.)

One of the most interesting examples of government activity in the field of language planning and language standardization is provided by modern Norway. There are in Norway today two official standard Norwegian languages. On the face of it this is a rather strange state of affairs for a country of less than four million inhabitants. The two standards are known as Nynorsk ('new Norwegian') and Bokmål ('book language') – neither of them particularly apt names – and both have equal official status. (In other words the relationship is not a diglossic one in the sense of Chapter 5.) Bokmål is the language of the national press (although some newspapers include articles in Nynorsk), of a majority of books, particularly translations, and of a majority of schoolchildren, as the medium of education. Nynorsk is used in the local press, particularly in the west of the country; it is the school language of about 20 per cent of children; and it is used in much poetry and literature, particularly in works with a rural background. All official documents are in both standards; children have to learn to read and write both; and both are extensively used in radio and television. In each area local councils decide which variety is to be used in public notices, and the standard to be used in each school district is also decided by democratic procedures.

Linguistically speaking the two are very similar, and they are totally mutually comprehensible. The dichotomy, moreover, applies much more to the written standard languages than to the spoken language. Most people speak rural dialects or non-standard urban dialects, although western dialects do tend to resemble Nynorsk more closely, and some eastern dialects are more similar to Bokmål. Perhaps sociolinguistically more interesting than the differences *between* the two languages, however, are the differences *within* them. In both Bokmål and Nynorsk there are variants (alternative words, pronunciations and grammatical constructions) which are known as *radical* and *conservative*. In the case of Bokmål, right-wing newspapers tend to use conservative forms, and left-wing papers radical forms. It is also often possible to make an intelligent guess about an educated speaker's politics from the forms he uses. This involvement of language with politics, in a rather unusually overt form, means that few Norwegians are very objective about the linguistic situation in their country, and that the 'language question' is often very hotly debated indeed. The heat of the argument can be judged from the fact that in 1955 a weather-forecaster on the Norwegian radio became known as the 'abominable snowman' and was actually dismissed because he refused to say *snø* (a radical Bokmål form) 'snow' instead of *sne* (a conservative form).

This Norwegian situation is clearly unusual, and, many Norwegians would say, a very awkward one, because it is expensive in a country with such a small population to print school books and official documents in both languages, and time-consuming for schools to have to teach both. In my own view it is in many ways a very good situation, since it means that far more Norwegians than would otherwise be the case are able to learn to read and, if they wish, write, speak and express themselves in a standard language that closely resembles their own native variety (dialectal variation being quite considerable in Norway). Far fewer Norwegian children therefore find themselves in the difficult situation of the Lowland Scots or Black English speaker.

It is interesting to trace the development of this situation because, although it is unique in Europe, it is nonetheless indicative of the type of language-planning activity in which governments can participate. Norway was ruled by Denmark from the fifteenth century until 1814. During this time the only official language was Danish, with the result that Norwegian dialects became heteronomous with respect to standard Danish. This was only possible, of course, because Danish resembled Norwegian quite closely. When independence from Denmark was won in 1814 there was therefore no specifically Norwegian standard language. A small number of immigrants actually spoke Danish, which was also used in the theatre, while the formal language of native government officials was in effect Danish with a Norwegian pronunciation. This was also how reading was taught in schools. The informal speech of upper-class speakers was a kind of compromise between this and local varieties: it was a fairly uniform kind of Danish-influenced Norwegian. Lower-class speakers in towns spoke Norwegian dialects perhaps somewhat influenced by Danish, whereas peasants and farmers spoke rural Norwegian dialects.

Two distinct responses were made to growing feelings in the country in favour of establishing a national Norwegian language. One strategy was to revise Danish gradually in the direction of the language of those upper-class urban people who spoke the Danish-influenced Norwegian. This Dano-Norwegian came to be known as Riksmål ('state language'), and was the forerunner of Bokmål. The other response was advocated by Ivar Aasen, a school teacher who had made an extensive study of Norwegian dialects. He advocated a more revolutionary approach, and devised a language of his own based on his dialect studies. The language was based on those rural dialects, mainly those of the West, which Aasen thought to be least 'contaminated' by Danish, and was called Landsmål ('language of the country'), which later became Nynorsk. In 1885, in response to various nationalist sentiments, Landsmål was made an official language on a par with Danish (or Riksmål). The government, however, did not feel free to abolish Dano-Norwegian because this was still the language of the influential urban elite. In fact, the position of Dano-Norwegian was strengthened when teachers were instructed, in 1887, not to teach the reading pronunciation of Danish but rather the colloquial standard, the modified Dano-Norwegian Riksmål. These two acts were the government's first involvement in language planning.

The origin of the conservative and radical forms in the two official languages today lies in the desire of successive governments to establish one national language instead of two without actually abolishing either of them. Rather the desire has been to reform the two gradually towards each other. For example, Norwegian dialects, including those of the urban working-class, have three genders for nouns (masculine, feminine and neuter), whereas Dano-Norwegian, subsequently Riksmål, had, like Danish, only two (common and neuter). This meant that Riksmål had identical forms for the definite article (which in Norwegian is placed after the noun) for masculine and feminine words: *mann* 'man', *ko* 'cow'; *mannen* 'the man', *koen* 'the cow'. Landsmål had distinct forms: *kui* 'the cow'. In 1917 the government introduced an official reform, one of the effects of which was to achieve a compromise between the two languages on this (and other) points. In Landsmål the form of the feminine definite article was to be changed from -*i* to -*a* to bring it into line with eastern dialects, while in Riksmål the feminine form -*a* was introduced obligatorily for some words, particularly words with rural associations, like *cow*, and optionally for others. This meant that 'the cow' was now *kua* in both languages. ('Obligatory' here means obligatory in school textbooks and in schoolchildren's writing.) As a result of this reform the feminine definite article used in conjunction with some nouns in Bokmål is considered to be a radical form, the masculine (or common) article a conservative form.

The next important development in government language planning was the 1938 reform, which was based on the report of a committee whose mandate was 'to bring the two languages closer together with respect to spelling, word-forms, and inflections, on the basis of the Norwegian folk language'. They were thus specifically instructed *not* to model the standard languages on the speech of the educated upper classes, an unusual and important step in the history of language standardization. Major changes that were to be made in Bokmål schoolbooks were the introduction of diphthongs for monophthongs in many words, as in Nynorsk and many dialects:

> *øst* > *aust* 'east' cf. Danish *øst*
> *sten* > *stein* 'stone' cf. Danish *sten*

and a change in the past tense endings of verbs from *-et* to *-a*, again as in many lower prestige eastern dialects, rural dialects, and Nynorsk:

> *vaknet* > *vakna* 'woke up'

The implementation of these reforms was delayed by the war, but after the war schoolbooks began to be issued in the new standards. The changes in Bokmål provoked angry reactions on the part of upper-class speakers, and many middle-class speakers in the East. Many parents, particularly in Oslo, felt these new forms to be vulgar, and objected to the fact that the same forms they had tried to 'correct' in their children's speech were now actually appearing in print. During the early 1950s, therefore, large business concerns and conservative politicians financed widespread campaigns against the reforms. Tremendous controversy ensued, and it was against this background that the 'abominable snowman' incident took place.

In spite of this opposition, a new Language Commission was set up with the same mandate as the committee that had produced the 1938 report, in order to supervise schoolbook norms for the two languages. (Right-wingers regarded the commission as representing the 'legalization of vulgarity', left-wingers a 'victory for democracy'.) In 1959 these schoolbook norms were published, and turned out to be basically the same as the 1938 forms, although not so radical. As a result of their recommendations there are now three different types of form in schoolbooks, in both Bokmål and Nynorsk; *obligatory* forms (only one possibility permitted); *alternative* forms (two possibilities permitted); and *optional* forms (not permitted in print, but children can use them in their own writing). Speakers and writers of the two Norwegians therefore have a considerable amount of choice open to them, in many ways a very good thing.

Specific proposals made by the commission were that the feminine definite article in Bokmål should be obligatory with a rather smaller number of nouns; the number of past-tense forms where -*a* was obligatory was sharply reduced and -*a* and -*et* were made alternatives; and diphthongs became obligatory in fewer words. A diphthong, for example, is obligatory in *sein* 'late' (although conservative newspapers still write *sen*); an alternative in *beisk/besk* 'bitter'; an optional form in (*eid*)/*ed* 'oath'; and a monophthong is obligatory in *en* 'one' (*ein* is Nynorsk only). (Similarly, and more amusingly, *daud* 'dead' is all right for animals, but *død* should be used of people.) The following is useful for diagnosing the provenance of written publications in Bokmål:

	'the book'	'delayed'
political right	*boken*	*forsinket*
political left	*boka*	*forsinket*
many schoolbooks	*boka*	*forsinka*

The two sentences overleaf illustrate in greater detail the relationship between the two languages, as well as some of the differences within them. (Not all the forms used here are actually allowed in the schoolbook norms, but most of them can be found in printed works of various kinds. Some of the 'radical' forms are much more 'radical' than others, and no attempt has been made to preserve stylistic consistency in any of the versions.)

(A final footnote on the Norwegian linguistic scene: Norway actually has two names in Norwegian, *Noreg* in Nynorsk, and *Norge* in Bokmål.)

	When	she	awoke	the morning	after,	felt	the town	under	the raw-cold	winter clouds	even more	dreary	than	ary	time	before.	It was	because	she	had
Conservative Nynorsk:	Då	ho	vakna	morgonen	etter,	kjendest	byen	under dei	råkalde	vinterskyene	enda	trøysteslaus	enn	noken	gong	før.	Det var	av di	ho	hadde
Moderate Nynorsk:	Da	ho	vakna	morgonen	etter,	kjendest	byen	under dei	råkalde	vinterskyene	enda	trøysteslaus	enn	noken	gong	før.	Det var	fordi	ho	hadde
Radical Nynorsk:	Da	ho	vakna	morgonen	etter,	kjendest	byen	under dei	råkalde	vinterskyene	enda meir	trøysteslaus	enn	noken	gong	før.	Det var	fordi	ho	hadde
Radical Bokmål:	Da	hun	vakna (vaknet)	morgenen	etter,	føltes	byen	under de	råkalde	vinterskyene	enda mer	trøsteslaus	enn	noen	gang	før.	Det var	fordi	hun	hadde
Moderate Bokmål:	Da	hun	vaknet	morgenen	etter,	føltes	byen	under de	råkalde	vinterskyene	enda mer	trøstesløs	enn	noen	gang	før.	Det var	fordi	hun	hadde
Conservative Bokmål:	Da	hun	våknet	morgenen	efter,	føltes	byen	under de	råkalde	vinterskyer	enda mer	trøstesløs	enn	noen	gang	før.	Det var	fordi	hun	hadde
(literal translation)	When	she	awoke	the morning	after,	felt	the town	under	the raw-cold	winter clouds	even more	dreary	than	ary	time	before.	It was	because	she	had

	another world	to	compare	it	with:	that	world	which
Cons. Nn.:			samanlikna	honom			verdi	
Mod. Nn.:			samanlikna	han			verda	
Rad. Nn.:	ei anna verd	å	samanlikne	han	med:	den	verda	som
Rad. Bm.:	ei anna verd	å	sammenlikne	den	med:	den	verda	som
Mod. Bm.:	en annen verden		sammenligne	den			verden	
Cons. Bm.:	en annen verden		sammenligne	den			verden	som

	lived within	him,	the	fine	cities	which	shone	out
Cons. Nn.:	budde inne	honom,						
Mod. Nn.:		han,						
Rad. Nn.:	budde inne	i han,	dei	vakre	storbyane	som	lyste	ut
Rad. Bm.:	budde inne	i han,	de	vakre	storbyene	som	lyste	ut
Mod. Bm.:	bodde inne	ham,			storbyene	som		
Cons. Bm.:	bodde inne	ham,			storbyer			

	from his	eyes
Cons. Nn.:	or	augo
Mod. Nn.:	av	auga
Rad. Nn.:	av	auga
Rad. Bm.:	av	øyene hans.
Mod. Bm.:	av	øynene hans.
Cons. Bm.:	hans	øyne.

from his eyes ('eyes-the his' in all except Cons. Bm.).

7. Language and Geography

We saw in Chapter 2 that there is a relationship in Britain between social dialects and geographical dialects such that regional linguistic differentiation is greatest at the level of varieties most unlike standard English. The social and linguistic reasons for the development of regional differences of this type are complex, and by no means completely understood. They are clearly the result of language changing in different ways in different places, but the actual process of linguistic change is something we know very little about.

Earlier on in this book, we briefly discussed the importance, in the development of regional dialects, of geographical features such as barriers and distance. When a linguistic innovation – a new word, a new pronunciation, a new usage – occurs at a particular place, it may subsequently spread to other areas, particularly those nearest to it, so long as no serious barriers to communication intervene. If an innovation started in London, we would expect to find that it later began to be used in Cambridge before it found its way into the speech of Carlisle. It might, though, take considerably longer to reach Belfast, because of the Irish Sea. This is an obvious point, and one that does not apply only to language. All technological and behavioural innovations are subject to the same processes. When mini-skirts were becoming fashionable, studies showed that girls were generally wearing their skirts shorter in London than they were in Newcastle where, in turn, they were shorter than those worn in Edinburgh.

The social and geographical pressures involved in the diffusion of linguistic innovations are of course a good deal more complex than those associated with fashions. It is possible, however, to demonstrate in a broad kind of way that similar factors are at work. A good example of a linguistic innovation which has been subject to this kind of process is the loss in English of postvocalic /r/ in works like *cart* and *car* which we discussed in Chapter 1. Map 1 is based on the survey of conservative rural dialects carried out under the direction of Harold Orton at the University of Leeds, and shows those areas of England where loss of post-vocalic /r/ in the pronunciation of the words *farm* or *yard* has not yet taken place. If we did not know already from other sources (such as the spelling) that it is the form without /r/ which is the newer, the separation of the three relatively peripheral areas shown on the map (the south-west, the north-west, and the north-east, spreading up into Scotland) would suggest most strongly that this was the case. (An identical innovation is unlikely to start in three separate areas at once.) The configuration of r-pronouncing areas on the map also suggests that the innovation began some-where in the centre or east of England before spreading north and west, although we cannot be certain, from the map alone, *when* the innovation began.

Sociolinguistically speaking, this map represents a considerable simplification of the true state of affairs concerning postvocalic /r/ in England. First, it is confined to only two words: an ex-amination of data for other words would reveal additional areas, such as parts of east Yorkshire, where postvocalic /r/ may be pronounced. Secondly, it is socially very incomplete. All along the eastern edge of the south-western area, for instance, it is only older speakers from the lowest social groups who are 'r-pro-nouncers', and even they are likely to use an r less frequently and pronounce it less strongly than speakers further south and west. Thirdly, the map gives information only for rural linguistic varieties. For many urban areas, particularly the larger towns, the impression given is very inaccurate since, unlike the rural areas, they may be entirely 'r-less' (this is true of Liverpool, for example).

The reason for this difference between urban and rural accents is that linguistic innovations, like other innovations, often spread from one urban centre to another, and only later spread out into

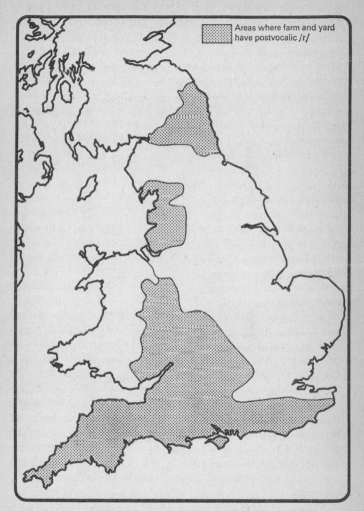

Map 1. Postvocalic /r/ in yard *and* farm *in conservative rural dialects in England*

the surrounding countryside. This is due to the general economic, demographic and cultural dominance of town over country, and to the structure of the communication network. The spread of linguistic features from one area to another is therefore not dependent solely on proximity. An innovation starting in London is quite likely to reach Bristol before it reaches rural Wiltshire, although the latter is nearer. The speech of Manchester, too, is in many ways more like that of London than of nearby rural Cheshire:

	London	Manchester	Hyde, Cheshire
'brush'	[brʌš]	[brəš]	[brəiš]
'such'	[sʌč]	[səč]	[sɪč]
'tough'	[tʌf]	[təf]	[tɒf]
'put'	[pʊt]	[pət]	[pər]

The Manchester and London forms are not identical, but there is a regular relationship such that all London [ʌ] and [ʊ] vowels correspond to Manchester [ə] vowels. In the case of the Hyde forms there is no such regular correspondence.

Distance, then, is clearly an important factor in the spread of linguistic forms, although in many cases social distance may be as important as geographical distance, as we have just seen: two towns may be socially 'closer' to each other than they are to the intervening stretches of countryside. What of barriers? We mentioned, in Chapter 2, the role of social barriers in the formation of social-class dialects, and the way in which the River Humber had acted as a geographical barrier to the spread of linguistic features in the north of England. There is also a third type of barrier which surprisingly enough does not necessarily have a significant slowing-down effect – namely the *language barrier*. Linguistic innovations, it appears, spread not only from one regional or social variety of the same language to another; they *may* also spread from one language into another.

An interesting example of a linguistic feature that has spread in this way is the European *uvular r*. It is thought that up until at least the sixteenth century all European languages had an r-type sound which was pronounced as r still is pronounced today in many types of Scots English or Italian: a tongue-tip trill (roll) or flap. At some stage, though, perhaps in the seventeenth century, a new pronunciation of r became fashionable in upper-class Parisian French. This new r, uvular r [R], is pronounced in the back of the mouth by means of contact between the back of the tongue and the uvula – technically a uvular trill, flap, fricative or frictionless continuant sound – and is the type of r sound taught today to foreign learners of French and German. Starting from this limited social and geographical base, the uvular-r pronunciation has during the last 300 years spread, regardless of language boundaries, to many other parts of Europe, as Map 2 shows. It is now used by the overwhelming majority of urban or educated French speakers, and by most educated Germans. Some Dutch speakers use it, as do nearly all Danes, together with a majority in the south of Sweden and parts of the south and west of Norway. On the other hand, it is not used in Bavarian, Austrian or, for the most part, Swiss German, nor, except by a small minority, in Italian. (The uvular r is also a feature of local English accents in parts of Northumberland and Durham. It is not clear whether this phenomenon is connected to the continental pronunciation or not.)

Processes of this type generally, when they involve grammar and vocabulary as well as phonetics and phonology, can lead to the development of *linguistic areas*. This term is used to refer to areas where several languages are spoken which, although they are not necessarily very closely related, have a number of features in common, as a result of the diffusion of innovations across language boundaries. One of the most interesting areas of this kind in Europe is the Balkans, comprising Yugoslavia, Albania, Greece, Bulgaria and Rumania. The languages involved are Serbo-Croat, Macedonian and Bulgarian (all Slav languages), Rumanian (a Romance language), Greek, and Albanian. These are all Indo-European languages, but apart from the three Slav languages they are not closely related genetically. Over the centuries, they have acquired a number of common features sometimes known as 'Balkanisms' which mark some or all of them off from other (often more closely related) European languages.

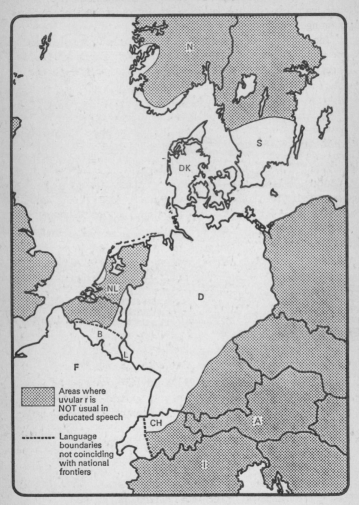

Map 2. Uvular r in Europe

Rumanian and Bulgarian, for example, have a number of common features which are not shared by any other Romance or Slav languages.

One of the most interesting features of the Balkan languages is the fact that four of them have a postposed definite article: the form corresponding to *the* in English is placed after the noun:

Albanian:	mekanik*u*
Bulgarian:	mexaniče*nut*
Macedonian:	mexaniča*rot*
Rumanian:	mecania*nul*
	'*the* mechanic'

(The only other European languages to have this feature are the Scandinavian languages.) Another grammatical feature shared by many of the Balkan languages is a particular usage of subordinate clauses. Most European languages employ a construction where English has:

> *They left without asking me*

which corresponds in English to:

> 'They left without to ask me.'

For example:

> 'They left . . . '
> French: . . . *sans me* demander
> German: . . . *ohne mich* zu fragen
> Danish: . . . *uden* at spørge *mig*.

In each case a construction with an infinitive can be used, although other constructions may be possible. In Albanian, Bulgarian, Greek, and Rumanian, on the other hand, another construction is usual, equivalent in English to:

> 'They left without that they asked me.'

For example:

> 'They left . . . '
> Bulgarian: . . . *bez da me popitat*
> Greek: . . . *xoris na me rotisune*
> ' . . . without that me they asked.'

Many other examples of linguistic areas can be found in different parts of the world. The Indian subcontinent is a good instance of an area where non-related languages have a number of features in common. Generally speaking, the majority of north Indian languages belong to the Indo-European family, while most of the languages spoken in the south of India are Dravidian. As far as we know, these language groups are not related at all. However, in spite of this lack of relationship, many Indian languages from both groups have grammatical constructions in common, and share a number of features of pronunciation. One of the most striking phonetic similarities is the presence in both families of retroflex consonants: consonants formed by curling the tip of the tongue back and bringing it into contact with the back of the alveolar ridge. (Consonant articulations of this type are a noticeable feature of the English pronunciation of speakers from the Indian subcontinent.) For example:

Dravidian languages	Tamil:	/koḍai/	'umbrella'
	Coorg:	/kaḍi/	'bite'
Indo-European languages	Marathi:	/ghoḍa/	'horse'
	Hindi:	/gaːḍi/	'cart'

Another comparable example is provided by certain of the languages of southern Africa, comprising several different Bushman and Hottentot languages, which may be related to each other, although this is far from certain, and a number of Bantu languages (which are definitely not related to Bushman and Hottentot) including Sotho, Zulu and Xhosa. These languages have a number of phonetic features in common, notably the presence of 'clicks' as consonants. ('Clicks' include sounds like that represented in English orthography as *tut-tut*, as well as the clicking noise made, in Britain at least, to encourage horses.) The letter *x* in Xhosa, incidentally, represents one particular type of click sound.

Linguistic innovations, then, can spread from one dialect into another adjacent dialect. If spreading of this type takes place across language boundaries, on a sufficiently large scale, linguistic areas are formed. Broadly speaking, though, it appears that only grammatical and phonological features require geographical proximity before diffusion of this sort can take place. (Uvular r can now be found in Norway, but it almost certainly arrived there from France via Germany and Denmark.) Lexical items appear to be able to spread across much greater distances. Words can be borrowed from one language into another regardless of proximity. Very often, when speakers of a particular language happen to be dominant in some particular field, other language groups adopt words pertaining to the field from this language. For example, many English musical terms – like *adagio*, *allegro*, *crescendo* – are of Italian origin, while sporting terms in many languages, like *football*, *goal*, *sprint*, as well as terms connected with pop music and jazz, tend to be English. At present, English is a source of loan words for very many languages, particularly in Europe. Borrowings of this type take place initially through the medium of the bilingual individual (there must be somebody who knows the foreign word in the first place), and individuals bilingual in English along with their native language are becoming increasingly common as the result of the widespread use of English as a lingua franca and its correspondingly widespread teaching in schools. This, of course, is not due to any inherent superiority of the English language as a medium of international communication, but rather to the former world political, economic, educational and scientific dominance of Britain and the similar present dominance of the USA.

The use of English as a lingua franca brings us to a rather diffcrent aspect of the geographical spread of linguistic phenomena. So far, we have confined our attention to those cases where features of a language can spread from person to person, group to group, and eventually, by this means – as in the case of uvular r – 'travel' over very large distances. Another equally important method by means of which linguistic forms may spread is for the speakers themselves to travel. (Uvular r might have arrived in Norway much sooner if large numbers of Parisians had emigrated to Norway, or had had extensive trade contacts there.) When, as the result of travel, speakers of different languages come into contact with each other, they may have to communicate by means of a lingua franca (see p. 145). Now, when English is used as a lingua franca in Europe, as it often is if, say, a Dutchman and a Swede want to talk to one another, it is frequently spoken with a great deal of fluency and expertise, usually as a result of many years' formal tuition in schools. Even so, it is still rather unusual to find a non-native speaker who uses English as a lingua franca who can speak English as well, and use it in as many different social situations, as a native English speaker. In other words, when a language is used as a lingua franca it normally undergoes a certain amount of simplification, and a reduction in (social) function – as well as being subject to the introduction of errors through interference from the native language of the speaker, or through imperfect learning.

Simplification and reduction in function of this kind may be slight (as perhaps in the case of educated Dutchmen and Swedes). On the other hand, where little or no formal schooling has taken place, it may be much larger; and where learning takes place only through intermittent and limited contacts, it may be very great indeed. This point can be illustrated from the case of Swahili, which, as we have seen, is widely used as a lingua franca in East Africa. On parts of the coast of East Africa, Swahili is the native language of many of the population who use it for all or most purposes and, naturally enough, speak it very fluently. Inland in Tanzania it is not widely spoken natively, but it is used to a considerable extent as a lingua franca. Compared to the coastal Swahili this inland lingua-franca variety demonstrates some features of simplification, since it is spoken as a second language, and it is subject to a reduction in function, for it is used in a more restricted set of circumstances than on the coast. Further inland still, in eastern Zaïre, yet another variety of Swahili is used as a lingua franca. In this case, even more simplification has taken place. 'Simplification' is a somewhat vague term and one which it is rather difficult to define, but the features of the Zaïre lingua-franca Swahili which the term is intended to cover include, in comparison to coastal Swahili, the absence of irregular verbs, the reduction in the number of noun classes (genders), and the avoidance of certain complex syntactic structures. Both these lingua-franca varieties of Swahili, although modified, are clearly nevertheless to be counted as Swahili. They are intelligible to coastal Swahili speakers, apparently, and native speakers of Swahili do not have to make very many concessions when talking to lingua-franca users in order to make themselves understood.

However, in another part of Zaïre, in the rural north, a further lingua-franca form of Swahili occurs. This variety again is simplified, relative to coastal Swahili, but much more so. Verb structures, for example, are radically simplified, there are no noun classes, and only a relatively limited number of sentence structures is employed. The result of this degree of simplification, it is said, is that mutual intelligibility with coastal Swahili is minimal. The language is used only as a lingua franca, yet if native Swahili speakers want to employ it as such they have to *learn* it – at least to a certain extent. When simplification has taken place on this scale, and when the result is a relatively stabilized form of language consistently employed as a lingua franca, the resulting variety is called a *pidgin* language (in this case we could call it Zaïre Pidgin Swahili).

A pidgin language, then, is a lingua franca which has no native speakers. Chronologically speaking, it is derived from a 'normal' language through simplification: most often reduction in vocabulary and grammar, and elimination of complexities and irregularities. There is also usually a certain amount of admixture, often considerable, from the native language or languages of those who use it, especially so far as pronunciation is concerned. Normally, in the first stages of its development at least, it is used only in trading or other limited-contact situations. (Where contacts are more permanent, fuller second-language learning is more likely to result.)

The most likely setting for the crystallization of a true pidgin language is probably a contact situation of this limited type involving three or more language groups: one 'dominant' language (in the case we have just discussed, Swahili), and at least two 'non-dominant' languages. If contact between the speakers of the dominant language and the others is minimal, and the imperfectly learned dominant language is then used as a lingua franca among the non-dominant groups, it is not difficult to see how a pidgin might arise. (The same sort of development might well take place if a Swedish schoolchild and a Dutch schoolchild, each with one year's study of English, were marooned alone on a desert island: they would probably develop a Dutch–Swedish Pidgin English as their mode of communication.) Moreover, it is possible that certain universal processes of simplification may play a part in the formation of pidgins. We shall discuss this last point briefly below.

It is important to realize that pidgins, although rather different from other languages, are really different in degree rather than in kind. They are genuine languages with structure and most of the attributes of other languages. They are difficult to learn properly, although probably easier than other languages (particularly for speakers of the languages dominant in their formation). Pidgins are not, therefore – as has often been maintained – haphazard mixtures, nor are they 'bad', 'debased' or 'corrupt' forms of the language from which they are derived. Consider the following example of British Solomon Islands Pidgin, often known as Neo-Solomonic by linguists, which is widely used as a lingua franca in the Solomon Islands:

Mifɛlə i-go go lɔŋ sɔlwater, lʊkautɪm fɪš, nau wɪn i-kəm. Nau mifɛlə i-go ɔləbaut lɔŋ kinú, nau bɪgfɛlə wɪn i-kəm nau, mifɛlə i-fafasi ɔləbautə, rɔŋ tuməs.

'We kept going on the sea, hunting for fish, and a wind arose. Now we were going in canoes, and an immense wind arose now, and we were thrown around and were moving very fast.'

Clearly, if one regards this as a form of English, then it is a very strange kind of English indeed. It is difficult to understand for an English speaker, particularly when heard rather than read, and the translation is necessary, I think. Similarly, if it is regarded as the result of an attempt by the speaker to learn English as a foreign language, then it is a very unsuccessful attempt. However, strictly speaking it is neither of those things. The speaker here *has* learnt a second language, but the second language he learnt was

Neo-Solomonic, not English. The grammar and vocabulary of Neo-Solomonic, although similar to English in many ways, is nonetheless quite distinct. The language has grammatical rules and words of its own. For example, *kaikai*, Neo-Solomonic for 'food, eat' is not an English word; and the requirement that transitive verbs be distinguished from intransitives (by the suffix – *ım* – compare *lokautım* with *go*) is not a grammatical rule of English. It is therefore quite desirable, on linguistic grounds alone, to regard Neo-Solomonic, and other varieties of Pidgin English, as languages quite separate from English (although obviously related to it). Another good, social, reason for doing this is that many people have objected to pidgins on the grounds that they have corrupted the 'purity' of English (or some other European language). Views like this are often accompanied by sentiments about racial and cultural 'purity' as well. If one regards a pidgin as a debased and inferior form of English, it may be quite easy to regard its speakers, mostly non-Europeans, as also being 'debased' and 'inferior'. One point that a linguist can make when faced with views such as these is to point out that there is no such thing as a 'pure' language. All languages are subject to change, and they are all the product of influence and admixture from other languages. (Take vocabulary alone: of the fifteen different words in my previous sentence, seven have been borrowed by English from foreign languages during the past 1,000 years.)

Most of the better-known pidgin languages in the world are the result of travel on the part of European traders and colonizers. They are based on languages like English, French and Portuguese, and are located on the main shipping and trading routes. English-based pidgins were formerly found in North America, at both ends of the slave trade in Africa and the Caribbean, in New Zealand and in China. They are still found in Australia, West Africa, the Solomon Islands (as we have seen) and in New Guinea, where Pidgin English is often called Neo-Melanesian by linguists. (Not all pidgin languages have arisen in this way, though. Kituba, which is derived from Kikongo, a Bantu language, is a pidgin widely used in western Zaïre and adjoining areas.

And Fanagolo, which is based on Zulu, is a pidgin spoken in South Africa and adjoining countries, particularly in the mines. There are several other indigenous pidgins in Africa and elsewhere.)

Neo-Melanesian is probably the most widely spoken pidgin derived from English. It has official status in New Guinea, and is used there on the radio, in newspapers, and in schools. At present in fact, it appears to be undergoing quite considerable *creolization*. As we saw in Chapter 3, creole languages are pidgins that have acquired native speakers. In linguistically mixed communities where a pidgin is used as the lingua franca, children may acquire it as their native language, particularly if their parents normally communicate in the pidgin. When this occurs – i.e., when creolization begins to take place – the language will re-acquire all the characteristics of a full, non-pidgin language. As spoken by an adult native speaker the language will have, when compared to the original pidgin, an expanded vocabulary, a wider range of syntactic possibilities, and an increased stylistic repertoire. It will also, of course, be used for all purposes in a full range of social situations. Creole languages, in other words, are perfectly normal natural languages – only their history is somewhat unusual.

Of European-based creole languages – those that have developed out of pidgins based on European languages – the best known are French, English, Portuguese and Spanish creoles. French creoles are widely spoken in the Caribbean and adjoining areas: Haiti, where Haitian French Creole is the native language of the vast majority of the population; Trinidad and Grenada, and other islands in the southern Caribbean; French Guiana; and the United States, where a French creole is spoken by Negroes in parts of Louisiana. French creoles are also spoken in the Indian Ocean, notably in Mauritius and the Seychelles. The following extract from the Lord's Prayer in Haitian Creole indicates the extent of the relationship between this creole and French:

Papa nou, ki nan sièl, ké non ou jouinn tout réspè. Ké règn ou vini. Ké volonté ou akonpli sou tè a tankou nan sièl. Ban nou, jodi a, pin chak jou nou.

Most of the better-known English creoles are spoken in different parts of the American continent and, like the French creoles, are a consequence of the slave trade. Sranan, for example, is an English creole spoken by several tens of thousands of native speakers in coastal areas of Surinam (Dutch Guiana), and is also widely used by others in the area as a lingua franca. Here is an example (see also p. 75):

Ala den bigibigi man de na balkon e wakti en. A kon nanga en buku na ondro en anu. A puru en ati na en ede, en a meki kosi gi den. Dan a waka go na a djari, pe den gansi de.

'All the important men were on the balcony waiting for him. He came with his book under his arm. He took off his hat and bowed before them. Then he went to the garden where the geese were.'

Sranan is one of the most 'conservative' of English creoles, i.e. it has been very little affected by influence from English, and it gives us a good idea of what other less isolated creoles may have been like at earlier stages of their history.

Inland in Surinam other English creoles, known collectively as 'Bush Negro', are spoken, mainly by the descendants of runaway slaves who succeeded in fleeing into the jungle. The best known of these creoles – which are apparently not intelligible to Sranan speakers – is Djuka. Just to make things more complicated, Djuka is apparently also spoken in pidginized form as a lingua franca by groups of Amerindians living in the area. This last variety has therefore had a history something like this:

English
  ↓   (pidginization)
West African Pidgin
  ↓   (creolization)
Djuka
  ↓   (pidginization)
Pidgin Djuka

Both Sranan and Djuka are uncontroversial, socially and linguistically. They are recognized by all to be creoles, and as languages distinct from English: it would be difficult to make out a good case for the above specimen of Sranan as a type of English. Mutual intelligibility between Sranan and English is nil. Socially, too, there are no reasons for regarding Sranan as a form of English. Dutch is the official language in Surinam, and English itself is little used. In other parts of the world, however, the position is much less clear. In parts of West Africa, for instance, Pidgin English is widely employed as a lingua franca, and in certain areas, notably in parts of Nigeria, it has become creolized. The difficulty there is that, in contrast to Surinam, English is an official language and is used, as a 'world language' of high prestige, in many different functions throughout the country. The result of this is that Nigerian Pidgin, even in its creolized form, has become heteronomous (see p. 16) with respect to standard British and/or Nigerian English. Pidgin English is subject to considerable influence from English, and is widely considered simply to be a 'bad' or 'corrupt' form of English. In Sierra Leone the situation is similar, although if anything rather more complicated. In Freetown, the capital, it is possible, probably somewhat artificially, to distinguish between four different linguistic varieties which have some connection with English:

1. British English;
2. Sierra Leone English – spoken mainly by middle-class Sierra Leonians, and containing certain features due to the influence of African languages;
3. West African Pidgin English – used as a (mainly commercial) lingua franca;
4. Krio.

Krio is an English creole with about 30,000 native speakers living in and around Freetown. The language has probably developed from an English creole spoken by slaves returned from Jamaica and from Britain, and is not directly connected with West African Pidgin. The following four versions of the same sentence illustrate some of the similarities and differences involved:

British English:	/aɪm goʊɪŋ tə wɜːk/
Sierra Leone English:	/aim goin to wɔk/
West African Pidgin:	/a di go wɔk/
Krio:	/a de go wok/

The similarities between the four varieties inevitably lead to the conclusion on the part of most Sierra Leonians that the three lower prestige forms represent unsuccessful attempts to imitate the higher prestige British English – and Pidgin and Krio in particular are often simply regarded as 'broken English'.

In parts of the formerly British West Indies the position is again similar, but the problems it brings with it are considerably more severe. Let us consider Jamaica. Some linguists writing about the language spoken in Jamaica refer to it as *Jamaican English* while others, preferring to give it the status of a separate language, call it *Jamaican Creole*. This disagreement about terminology is the result of the discreteness and continuity problem we mentioned in Chapter 1 (p. 16). In Jamaica, standard English is the official language and is spoken there, at the top of the social scale, by some educated Jamaicans and people of British origin. At the other end of the social scale, particularly in the case of peasants in isolated rural areas, the language used is an English-based creole which is not in itself mutually intelligible with standard English. The linguistic differences are great enough for us to be able to say, if these two varieties were the only two involved, that, like Sranan, Jamaican Creole is a language related to but distinct from English. To help make this point, here is an extract from a creole text cited by a Jamaican-Creole scholar, Beryl Bailey:

Wantaim, wan man en ha wan gyal-pikni nomo. Im ena wan priti gyal fi-truu. Im neba laik fi taak tu eni an eni man. Im laik a nais buosi man fi taak tu. Im taat taak tu wan man, bot im get kalops aafta im taak tu di man.

'Once upon a time, there was a gentleman who had an only daughter. She was a gay and dandy girl. She didn't like to talk to just any man. She wanted a gay, fine man to talk to. She started to talk to a man, but she got pregnant by talking to the man.' (Beryl Bailey's translation is into Jamaican rather than British standard English.)

The problem is, however, that between these two extremes, at intermediate points on the social scale, there is a whole range of intermediate varieties which connect the two in a chain of mutual intelligibility. There is, in other words, a social-dialect continuum ranging from standard English to 'deepest' Jamaican Creole. This means that all language varieties in Jamaica have become heteronomous with respect to standard English, even if they are not really mutually comprehensible with it. In fact the social-dialect continuum itself may have arisen in the first place – although this is not certain – as a result of the influence of high-prestige English on low-status Creole: the stronger the influence, the more 'decreolization' would take place. And the influence of English shows no sign of diminishing. Certainly, even 'deepest' Creole, as our text shows, is much more like English than Sranan is.

The problems caused by the English–Creole continuum in Jamaica are quite considerable. In Chapter 1, when we were talking about geographical dialect continua, we saw that, in the case of Dutch and German dialects, it was possible to make a (linguistically arbitrary) decision as to which varieties were dialects of which language, simply by using the political frontier. In Jamaica no equivalent 'social frontier' exists: we cannot place a clear dividing line between Creole and English. But if, as a consequence, we consider, as most people do, that the language of all Jamaicans is 'English', a number of problems may arise.

First, there is a very widespread view in Jamaica (as elsewhere in the Caribbean) that the majority of Jamaicans speak a very inferior type of English (since Jamaican Creole is obviously so different from English). Secondly, it means that children are taught to read and write in standard English; after all, 'English' is considered to be their language. Because of the great differences between English and many types of creole, however, many of these children never succeed in learning to read or write English with any degree of proficiency, and the failure rate of

Jamaican children taking British O-level and similar English examinations is very high, compared to their performance in other subjects.

From a purely linguistic point of view, a sensible solution to this state of affairs would be a Norwegian type of approach (forgetting for the moment that there are two standard Norwegians). In spite of the fact that standard Danish was similar to Norwegian dialects, to the extent that they were formerly felt to be heteronomous with respect to Danish, Norway developed its own standard language after political independence had been achieved. This new standard language was still similar to Danish, but was sufficiently different from it to make it resemble actual Norwegian speech much more closely. In Jamaica, and elsewhere, it would be possible to do the same sort of thing. A new standard Jamaican Creole (or English) could be developed that would reflect much more closely the nature of the language spoken by Jamaicans. It would resemble English, but would nevertheless be regarded as a different language. English could then be learnt later, once literacy had been acquired, as a semi-foreign language, much as Norwegians now learn to read and understand Danish and Swedish.

In practice, however, there are a great number of obstacles to a solution of this type. English is a statusful language which is also very useful as a lingua franca, and it is the language of a culture which is powerful and influential in Jamaica. The political and social relationship between Jamaican Creole and English is therefore not exactly the same as that which existed between Danish and Norwegian. Few nineteenth-century Norwegians would have been upset by statements to the effect that they did not speak Danish. On the other hand, many West Indians might feel insulted by suggestions that they do not speak English. This is because a) varieties near the (social) top of the Jamaican dialect continuum are much more like English than Creole – there is no real linguistic reason for saying they are 'not English', and b) it is a characteristic of social attitudes to language that they tend to be shared even by those who suffer most from those attitudes: standard English is accepted by nearly everybody in Jamaica as 'good' and deviations from it as 'bad'. Further, because of the prestige of standard English, those who have already mastered it would not readily relinquish the social and financial advantages it has brought them. People would be conscious, too, of the danger of becoming isolated from the rest of the English-speaking world. The main problem, though, would be one of people's social attitudes about the appropriateness of certain linguistic varieties to certain social contexts. To read the BBC news in a 'broad' London, Birmingham or Glasgow accent would provoke laughter, anger, and ridicule. The same kind of reaction could be expected to the introduction of Jamaican Creole into unexpected contexts. It could be done, however, if a political decision were made to do so: English would have sounded ridiculous in a law-court in the Middle Ages, and would have been considered out of place in a scientific treatise at a much later date than that; a piece of literature in Finnish would have been considered most unusual until comparatively recently; and the use of Macedonian as a parliamentary language would have been felt to be absurd until this century.

But if the linguistic reasons for teaching standard English in Jamaica are fairly weak, they are much stronger when it comes to the education of children of West Indian origin in Britain. Here there are very good grounds for arguing that West Indian children should learn to understand and read standard British English. At the same time, however, it is important for all those involved in educational work to realize that many West Indian children, particularly those newly arrived, may face very great difficulties of a semi-foreign-language nature. It is also important to point out that there is absolutely nothing wrong or inadequate about West Indian Creole as language. (Not the least of the children's problems *may* be being told that their language is 'broken', 'lazy' or 'gibberish'.) Teacher and pupil may have to *learn* to understand one another. Ideally this should be a two-way process – it is not enough simply to demand that the West Indian child speak 'good' (i.e. British) English. (One tragic result of the failure to appreciate the language problems of West Indian children in Britain is that an unduly high proportion of them have been classified as educationally subnormal. Their position is similar to that of many children who have been considered to be 'verbally deprived': instead of being regarded as linguistically *different* they are regarded as linguistically *deficient*.)

From a more theoretical linguistic point of view, one of the most interesting features of creole languages generally – at least in the case of those related historically to European languages – is the number of similarities they share with one another, regardless of geographical location. Consider the following verb forms:

Jamaican Creole:	/wa de go hapm nou/	'What's going to happen now?'
Sranan:	/mi de kom/	'I'm coming.'
Gullah:	/de də njam forə/	'They were eating fodder.'
Krio:	/a de go wok/	'I'm going to work.'

(Jamaican Creole is, geographically, Caribbean; Sranan, South American; Gullah [see also p. 75], North American; and Krio, West African.) The above sentences all demonstrate what can be called *progressive* or *continuous aspect*: they concern, not single short-lived actions, but actions taking place over a relatively longer period of time. (This is revealed in the English translations by verb forms with *be*+verb-*ing*.) The similarities to note are as follows:

1. All these creoles are able to mark continuous aspect without marking tense. (The Gullah example has been translated as past, but in other contexts it could equally well be present.)

2. All the creoles show continuous aspect, not by an inflection of the verb, as in English, but by a particle – an independent word standing before the verb.

3. The actual form of this particle is almost identical in each case: *de, de, də, de*.

These similarities are even more striking if we note that French-based creoles demonstrate exactly the same verb structure:

pronoun+continuous-aspect particle+verb

Louisiana FC: /   mo ape travaj/   'I am working.'
Haitian FC: /   yo ape măze/   'They are eating.'
Mauritius FC: /ki to   ape fer/   'What are you doing?'

Note, too, that once again the form of the particle is identical /ape/ (historically related to French *après*), in spite of the several thousand miles which separate Mauritius from the Caribbean. Note also that the presence of continuous aspect is rather more surprising in French creoles than in those derived from English since French itself does not have the distinction between *I ate it* and *I was eating it* that English does. Portuguese creoles, too, have the same construction:

St Thomas Portuguese Creole: /e ka nda/
                             pronoun+particle+verb =
                                     'He is going.'

How can we explain the similarities (both of structure and of form) between these languages, particularly in view of the great distances separating them and of the fact that they appear to be historically derived from different sources? One explanation that has been put forward stresses the similarity of those situations which led to the growth of pidgins (and hence of creoles). These languages were generally the joint creation of sailors, traders and indigenous peoples in trading or other similar contexts, it is pointed out, and it is therefore not surprising that these languages are similar. It is also true – and this may be a stronger argument – that pidgins grow up in circumstances where the transmission of information is very difficult and where it may be very useful to make language as simple and efficient an instrument of communication as possible. That is, there may be universal or widespread principles of simplification – including the loss of redundant features and the omission of irregularities – which will favour some structures more than others. Perhaps some grammatical structures are intrinsically easier to learn. Certainly the rule for the formation of the past tense in French creoles: 'Add the particle *te* before the verb' – appears to be much easier than the corresponding French rule:

Louisiana Creole:	/mo te pe kupe/	'I was cutting,'
Haitian Creole:	/yo te bwc/	'They drank.'

A second solution goes under the name of the 'relexification theory'. Briefly, this theory claims that the first widespread European-based pidgin was Portuguese Pidgin, which probably grew up some time during the fifteenth century along the West African coast. The Portuguese then spread it to their other trading posts and colonies in Africa and Asia, and traders from other countries began to learn it as well. However, when French and English traders entered the trade – particularly the slave trade – in large numbers, *relexification* of this Portuguese pidgin took place. The grammar of the language remained the same, but the *words* were changed. Words derived from Portuguese were gradually replaced by words from English, French, or some other dominant European language. The evidence in favour of this theory is as follows:

1. Some Portuguese words still remain in many non-Portuguese pidgins and creoles e.g. *savvy*, from Portuguese *sabe* 'he knows', and *piccaninny*, from Portuguese *pequenino*, 'little'.

2. A large number of words found in creole languages can be traced back to West African languages. For example, /njam/ 'eat', which is found in Jamaican Creole, Gullah, Sranan, and others, probably derives from /njami/, which means 'to eat' in Fulani, a language spoken today in Guinea, Gambia, Senegal and Mali.

3. There are a number of grammatical similarities, in addition to those we have already noted in the case of verbs, between English, French, Portuguese and other creoles. The 'same grammar but different words' hypothesis provides a ready explanation for this.

4. The actual nature of the grammatical similarities – although they may be partly due to universal principles of simplification – suggests links with West African languages. Many of these

languages, like the creoles, indicate aspect and tense by means of preposed particles, for instance. Compare:

Louisiana French Creole:	/mo to kupe/	'I (past) cut.'
St Thomas Portuguese Creole:	/e ta nda/	'He (past) go.'
Yoruba:	/mo ti wa/	'I (past) come.'

One final piece of evidence for the relexification hypothesis may be provided by Saramakkan. This is a creole language also spoken in Surinam. It appears that this creole may have been arrested, by the flight of the slaves who spoke it into the jungle, at a half-way stage of transfer from Portuguese- to English-derived vocabulary. It is most often considered to be a Portuguese creole, but the English element in the vocabulary is very large. In any case, whatever the explanation for the similarities between creoles, these languages provide a particularly fascinating example of the linguistic consequences that can follow from the social interaction in particular social contexts of different social, ethnic and language groups.

Annotated Bibliography and Further Reading

Chapter 1

The railway-carriage example illustrated the way in which language i) can give social clues about a speaker, and ii) is involved in the establishment of social relationships. In this book, ii) has not been treated at any length, and the gap can be filled by reference to J. Laver & S. Hutcheson, eds., *Communication in Face to Face Interaction* (Penguin). Similarly, the present book has concentrated more on sociological and geographical aspects of sociolinguistics. The balance can be restored by the more anthropological articles in J. Pride & J. Holmes, eds., *Sociolinguistics* (Penguin), and D. Hymes, ed., *Language in Culture and Society* (Harper & Row). The latter is a very useful source of bibliographical information, and contains, amongst many other important articles, a paper by Haas on interlingual taboo from which I have taken some of the data used here. Other useful introductory works include R. Burling, *Man's Many Voices* (Holt, Rinehart & Winston) – the full Njamal kinship data occurs in its most accessible form here, S. Lieberson, ed., *Explorations in Sociolinguistics* (Mouton) which contains Friedrich's study of Russian kinship terms, and P. Giglioli, ed., *Language and Social Context* (Penguin). The writings of Sapir and Whorf, both of which are highly recommended, are to be found in D. Mandelbaum, ed., *Selected Writings of Edward Sapir in Language, Culture and Personality* (California UP), and B. Whorf, *Language, Thought and Reality* (MIT Press). Much of the work by Labov referred to in this book can be found in W. Labov, *The Social Stratification of English in New York City* (Center for Applied Linguistics, Washington DC = CAL). The influence of Labov's work can be noted in much of the present book, and his writings are both stimulating and important. Collections of his articles are to appear quite soon, and papers by him can be found in most sociolinguistics readers.

Chapter 2

The results of the Detroit urban dialect survey led by Roger Shuy are not readily available in their entirety. Some of the results, however, including many of those I have used here, are set out in W. Wolfram, *A Sociolinguistic Description of Detroit Negro Speech* (CAL). The Norwich data can be found in P. Trudgill, *The Social Differentiation of English in Norwich* (Cambridge UP). Many of Bernstein's papers are now published together as B. Bernstein, *Class, Codes and Control*, vol. 1, (Routledge & Kegan Paul), while some of the arguments against the 'verbal deprivation' hypothesis can be found in W. Labov 'The Logic of Non-Standard English', an article which has now been reprinted in a number of places, including the Giglioli volume (in part), and R. Abrahams & R. Troike, eds., *Language and Cultural Diversity in American Education* (Prentice-Hall).

Chapter 3

W. Whiteley, ed., *Language Use and Social Change* (Oxford UP) contains a paper by Berry dealing with the Accra data, together with a number of other articles relevant to the topics discussed in Chapters 5 and 6. Readers interested in 'Black English' and associated educational problems are referred to three books published by the CAL: J. Baratz & R. Shuy, eds., *Teaching Black Children to Read*; R. Fasold & R. Shuy, eds., *Teaching Standard English in the Inner City*; and W. Wolfram & N. Clarke, eds., *Black–White Speech Relationships*. A more popular but well researched introduction is J. Dillard, *Black English* (Random House). American teachers and educationists are also referred to R. Burling's excellent *English in Black and White* (Holt, Rinehart & Winston).

Chapter 5

Brown & Gilman's T- and V-pronoun article, 'The Pronouns of Power and Solidarity', and Ferguson's 'Diglossia' paper have both been reprinted a number of times. The former appears in J. Fishman, ed., *Readings in the Sociology of Language* (Mouton), which is itself a very valuable collection of readings, and the latter in the Hymes reader. Both also appear in the Giglioli volume. For those especially interested in style and stylistics D. Crystal & D. Davy, *Investigating English Style* (Longman) is particularly recommended, while a number of articles in J. Gumperz & D. Hymes, eds., *Directions in Sociolinguistics* (Holt, Rinehart & Winston) deal with aspects of the relationship between language and social context.

Chapter 6

The discussion of language planning in Malaysia is taken from R. Le Page *The National Language Question* (Oxford UP). Many of the facts about the Norwegian situation can be found in a detailed and balanced treatment by E. Haugen, *Language Conflict and Language Planning: The Case of Modern Norwegian* (Harvard UP). J. Fishman *et al.*, eds., *Language Problems of Developing Nations* (Wiley) is another good source of information on problems of planning and standardization in different parts of the world.

Chapter 7

The English dialect data presented can be found in the publications of the *Survey of English Dialects* edited by H. Orton *et al.* and published by Arnold. The basic material is now all published and comes in four volumes, each in three parts (i.e. twelve books in all): I, The Six Northern Counties; II, The West Midland Counties; III, The East Midland Counties and East Anglia; and IV, The Southern Counties. (These are best consulted in libraries.) The Neo-Solomonic data is taken from R. Hall, *Pidgin and*

Creole Languages (Cornell UP), which is a good introduction to the subject, and contains an appendix with examples from several different pidgins and creoles. Bailey's data can be found in an article in D. Hymes, ed., *Pidginisation and Creolisation of Languages* (Cambridge UP). This is not an introductory work, but is important reading, particularly for theoretical aspects of this topic, and contains a very useful list of known pidgins and creoles compiled by I. Hancock. My 'Dutch–Swedish Pidgin English' example is based on a paper by Whinnom in the same volume.

Index

More about Penguins and Pelicans

Penguinews, which appears every month, contains details of all the new books issued by Penguins as they are published. From time to time it is supplemented by *Penguins in Print*, which is a complete list of all titles available. (There are some five thousand of these.)

A specimen copy of *Penguinews* will be sent to you free on request. For a year's issues (including the complete lists) please send 50p if you live in the British Isles, or 75p if you live elsewhere. Just write to Dept EP, Penguin Books Ltd, Harmondsworth, Middlesex, enclosing a cheque or postal order, and your name will be added to the mailing list.

In the U.S.A.: For a complete list of books available from Penguin in the United States write to Dept CS, Penguin Books Inc., 7110 Ambassador Road, Baltimore, Maryland 21207.

In Canada: For a complete list of books available from Penguin in Canada write to Penguin Books Canada Ltd, 41 Steelcase Road West, Markham, Ontario.

Linguistics

David Crystal

'It is impossible to conceive of a rational being, or of a society, without implying the existence of a language. Language and thinking are so closely related that any study of the former is bound to be a contribution to our understanding of the human mind.'

Popular interest and the evident importance of language as the principal means of communication between people, interests, creeds and nations have promoted linguistics, largely in this century from an amateur study to a widespread academic discipline.

David Crystal shows here what the benefits, as well as the problems, are in studying language in a scientific way. He places modern linguistics in historical perspective and traces in the present century six 'ages' in its development, each with its dominant, and abiding, theme. His central chapter discusses, one by one, phonetics, phonology, morphology, 'surface' syntax, 'deep' syntax, and lastly semantics.

Dr Crystal's book makes a novel and lively introduction to a significant subject which today concerns not only psychologists, sociologists and philosophers, but teachers, interpreters and even telephone companies.